Praise for Gary

"Gary Scott lives his life to the absolute fullest and climbs both literally and figuratively in a way that inspires an extraordinary legion of followers. It is hard to imagine a better guide."

—KIM AND DEMETRI COUPOUNAS,
COFOUNDERS OF GOLITE, BOULDER, COLORADO

"We all have an Everest to climb and master in our lives. This book gives the steps to take to help you overcome your doubts and fears and move closer to your dreams."

—DAVID BREASHEARS, LEADER AND CO-DIRECTOR
OF THE EVEREST IMAX FILMING EXPEDITION

"I can think of no one who couldn't benefit from reading *Summit Strategies.*"

—PETER ATHANS, TECHNICAL DEVELOPMENT FOR
THE NORTH FACE AND SEVEN TIMES EVEREST SUMMITER

"No matter what your goals are, *Summit Strategies* will help and inspire you to climb your personal Everest."

—ED WEBSTER, MOUNTAINEER AND AUTHOR OF
SNOW IN THE KINGDOM: MY STORM YEARS ON EVEREST

"Every person who is concerned about living life to its fullest ought to read this book. The life lessons are so simple, and yet at the same time, so profound."

—PASTOR RON L. VIETTI, VALLEY BIBLE FELLOWSHIP

"Gary Scott is a rock solid person—as stable as the mountains he has climbed. Listen to the ideas and principles in this book. They are true, forthright, and can apply in your own life."

—MICHAEL A. BOYLAN, AUTHOR OF *THE POWER TO GET IN*

SUMMIT STRATEGIES

▲

**Secrets to
Mastering the Everest
in Your Life**

SUMMIT STRATEGIES

▲

Secrets to
Mastering the Everest
in Your Life

Gary P. Scott

BEYOND
WORDS
Publishing
I N C

Beyond Words Publishing, Inc.
20827 N.W. Cornell Road, Suite 500
Hillsboro, Oregon 97124-9808
503-531-8700

Editor: Jenefer Angell
Managing editor: Julie Steigerwaldt
Copyeditor: David Abel
Design: Karen Schober
Composition: William H. Brunson Typography Services
Printed in the United States of America

Distributed to the book trade by Publishers Group West

Library of Congress Cataloging-in-Publication Data

Scott, Gary P.
    Summit strategies : secrets to mastering the Everest in your life /
  Gary P. Scott.
      p. cm.
    ISBN 1-58270-101-6
    1. Success.   2. Mountaineering—Miscellanea.   I. Title.
  BJ1611.2.S36   2003
  158.1—dc22

                                                    2003015295

The corporate mission of Beyond Words Publishing, Inc.:
  Inspire to Integrity

To my mom, my dad, my wife Diane,
and everyone who has a dream!

Trevor:

Never give up
on your dreams!

You've got tremendous
potential - don't
waste it!

My Best!

Gary Sirak

Contents

Acknowledgments

There are many people I would like to thank for making this book possible, and for being such a tremendous part of my life.

To my incredibly hard-working literary agent Pamela Harty, as well as Deirdre Knight and Lisa Payne at the Knight Agency—thank you for believing in this book from the start. To my phenomenal editor Jenefer Angell, who was a joy to work with, as well as Beth Hoyt, Sylvia Hayes, Julie Steigerwaldt, Karolyn Nearing, Dorral Lukas, and my publishers Cynthia Black and Richard Cohn at Beyond Words Publishing—thank you for having such faith in me and for all your hard work. You are an awesome team. And a huge thanks to my faithful and unstoppable editorial assistant Diana Pearson, who went way beyond the call of duty to make this book happen.

Thank you to the many friends who spent countless hours reading, rereading, and editing these stories and lessons, molding them into what's ahead, especially John Rodwick, Ph.D., Derek Patterson, Constance Gay, Debbie Henkins, Kelly Johnson, Dale Griffin, Gary Michael, Sue Breeze, Demetri and

Kim Coupounas, Jeff Mackler, and everyone else who read a chapter or two and gave me their input.

A special thanks to my old P.E. and English teacher George Simpkin, who believed in me from the start; to Reinhold Messner, who set the standards to which we all aspire; to Trevor Pilling, who taught me to laugh at myself; and to Pemba Tenzing Sherpa—no one could ask for a more loyal friend and guide. Thanks to Don Crawford Jr., W. Alan Gay, John Wiester, Ron Vietti, Steve Jolley, Dale Griffin, Gerry Lee, Bob Tretheway, Terry Felber, and Doug Storey for mentoring me, and to Stoney Mayock for being a true "mountaineer's" friend.

Thanks to everyone I've ever climbed with, especially Marc DeCure (with whom I did my very first climb), Simon Parker, Peter Hoffstetter, Mark Barnett, Greg Moore, Colin Reece, Kim Carrigan, Trevor Pilling, Roger Marshall, Bruce Hendricks, Dave Kelley, Pete Athans, Rick Wilcox, Marc Chauvin, Tommy Heinrich, Aron Ralston, Tracy Iverson, Gary Guller, and my mentor John Fisher, who taught me how to guide.

To my faithful writing companions DiDi and Makalu, our two Burmese cats; to my mother, my greatest fan and supporter, who let me do things no mother would want a son to do; to my dad, a man I aspire to emulate, who showed me the world and my first mountain; to my extended family, for always believing in this book, and me; and especially to my very supportive wife

Diane, who gave me the freedom to write and to be myself, and to go back to Everest for another attempt—thank you!

Thank you all, and forgive me for anyone I've forgotten (it's the altitude).

Now, go live your dreams!

Foreword

⌒

Gary Scott's *Summit Strategies* is a succinct and penetrating, even profound, analysis of what he has learned about himself—and, in turn, human nature—from living an extremely adventurous, physically demanding, risky, and spiritually rewarding life. I kept saying "Amen" to one piece of wisdom after another, on page after page. I marveled at how clearly and meaningfully he expressed his hard-earned strategies for climbing not only truly challenging, daunting, literal mountains, but also the most important and difficult one of all— every person's unique and figurative mountain of life.

Many self-improvement books are written by authors who are mostly spectators and academics but Gary has walked his talk. He stands out as an exceptionally qualified and completely believable spokesman for his convictions. In short, he is truly a life enhancer who obviously believes that to participate is to live and learning shared is multiplied.

I happen to have memorized many poignant and inspiring poems and aphorisms that I love dearly. I use these quotes daily as a conditioned reflex to cope with life's "downers" as well as to increase the joy of the "uppers." All through this book I was often reminded of these favorite and often-used standbys. Many of Gary's insights and perspectives will now be added to my mental mentoring method, for which I thank him deeply. And I expect that his other readers will do the same as everyone can find useful, timeless benefits within the pages of this very significant summary of Gary's mountain odyssey.

—Dick Bass
First summiter of the seven continental highs,
developer of Snowbird Ski and Summer Resort,
and co-author of *Seven Summits*

Introduction

THE STORY BEHIND THE LESSONS

At times grueling, even boring brother.

Keeping one step in front of the other;

But know beyond any doubt.

That's what success is all about.

—DICK BASS, "*FROM MY PERSPECTIVE*"

Mountains have been good to me. Over the past thirty-five years, climbing has taken me far and wide across our magnificent planet—extreme rock climbing all over Australia; alpine climbing across the United States; and guiding groups up Mount Aconcagua in South America, Kilimanjaro in Africa, Elbrus in Russia, and the volcanoes in Mexico. I've been on over thirty expeditions to the Himalayas, including successful trips to Mount Everest and Mount Kangchenjunga (the third highest peak in the world), plus many solo ascents and speed climbs of smaller peaks in Nepal and elsewhere.

When you spend a great deal of your life focused on one activity—especially one as mentally, physically, and emotionally demanding as Himalayan mountaineering; when you've lost more than two dozen friends to the mountains, and had to make life-and-death decisions over and over again, as quickly and easily as choosing what to have for lunch; you can't help but gain some valuable insights into life. Extreme adventures provide extreme lessons. Nature is an unforgiving classroom, and nowhere on earth are the forces of nature more unforgiving than in the highest mountains on the planet. From my experiences I have learned a great deal about myself, including how to set and achieve goals, how to overcome my doubts and fears, and how to achieve peak personal performance.

Contrary to popular belief, I do not have a death wish. I simply love climbing mountains. I've never felt more alive than when on a Himalayan peak heading for the summit. I joke that what I do best is carry a pack up steep snow slopes when there is no air and the weather is at its worst. The higher I get, the better I do, and the worse the weather, the better I like it. For people like me, climbing satisfies the need for accomplishment—that irresistible urge to challenge ourselves against nature and experience victory by getting to the top of something. All we have to do is overcome our doubts and fears to do it!

Mountaineering closely parallels other aspects of life, and that is why we can learn so much from it; there's a reason that holy men go to the mountains to find the meaning of life. I have experienced as many problems, weaknesses, and disappointments as anyone else, but my experiences in the mountains have taught me a unique way of dealing with what life throws at me. With this book I hope to impart some of what I have learned. The lessons formulate an "Everest Climber's Guide to Success," if you will. They have changed my life, and I'm confident that they can change yours.

Everyday life can be an incredible adventure when you truly challenge yourself. The stories and lessons in this book will help you discover and commit to your life's purpose with renewed passion, because you will be clearly reminded of the importance of staying true to yourself. With the reassurance of knowing that everyone, even a world-class mountaineer, faces fears, you will learn what you can do to control, manage, and overcome your own. You will see more clearly how the little decisions that you make affect the biggest results in every area of your life, and why it is vitally important, and to carefully choose who helps you achieve your ambitions, and to discover, acknowledge, and eliminate the obstacles that hold you back and the baggage that slows you down. As you identify and rise to your own standard of excellence, you will realize that what you learn—and what you become—while you pursue your goals is more important than actually achieving them.

Life can and should be an incredible adventure. It is of the utmost importance for all of us to follow our hearts, so that we can be true to our selves and live the life we were meant to live. Life shouldn't be measured by the work we do or the sport we play, but by who we are. I feel fortunate to have discovered the focus of my life at an early age, and I'm thankful that I chose to act upon that dream, but I know that many people are derailed from their deepest aspirations. Conflicting responsibilities, lack of encouragement, and any number of other interferences can get in the way. Fortunately, it's never too late to start, regardless of your age or how settled you are. All you need are some practical steps to help you reach the summits in all areas of your life.

Each chapter of *Summit Strategies* opens with a piece of the story of my first expedition to Mount Everest—a lifelong dream. The story captures my eager anticipation—and the overwhelming reality, as I battle for my life, lost in a raging blizzard at 26,000 feet, in the part of the mountain known as the "death zone," where the air is so thin that it barely sustains life. The insights gained from that experience represent the culmination of all the wisdom that I have gained from the mountains. The experiences of that expedition, and of the many others that I will share, are the foundation for this book; the simple lessons in each chapter, ten in all, serve as a sort of base camp from which you can set out on your own inner journey.

We are all climbers by nature, whether physically, professionally, or spiritually. As children, many of us are naturally attracted to climbing whatever we can; as we grow and find broader aspirations, that desire to ascend grows with us. We may go on to achieve great things, or we may find that something stops us from achieving our dreams. In climbing, the "crux" is the hardest move or section of a climb; in life, people experience cruxes with their health, their relationships, and their work. These cruxes are defining points at which we must decide to accept the challenge and move forward, or retreat. Many people turn back, out of habit. Over time, these retreats erode their self-confidence and belief in themselves, and they eventually stop trying. Of course, we have another, much more exciting option in these defining moments: we can confront the challenge, and keep moving forward.

Climbing—literal or otherwise—is an intellectual, emotional, and spiritual challenge. The strategies I put forth here are tools that will help you take the steps you need to realize any dream. The concepts are as straightforward as climbing is:

you get started and learn from whatever comes your way. As you climb, you conquer the smaller summits of doubts, fears, and insecurities—the obstacles that hold all of us back. I hold the world record for a one-day solo ascent of one of the coldest mountains on earth, Alaska's Mount McKinley, a record that has stood for seventeen years—but I didn't start there. In my climbing career, each lesson that I have learned has helped me to move to the next level of success.

Taking risks provides the building blocks to self-knowledge. This is true in climbing perhaps more than any other activity on earth. During a couple of hours of climbing you can experience more emotions than in a month of day-to-day life. Your senses are completely alert. A climb has a clear purpose and a clear outcome: either you reach the summit or you don't. You know whether you have made it, or if you backed down and cheated yourself out of your summit. The sharpness of the attendant insights has helped me spot the less dramatic, but no less important, milestones in life, when I'm not physically in the mountains. I have also seen how people achieve similar growth by challenging themselves in different arenas.

One of the things that sets climbing apart, and makes it so satisfying, is that only you can do it—no one else can do it for you. Climbing is dangerous, uncomfortable, demanding, stressful, frustrating, difficult, painful, lonely, sometimes boring and monotonous, and often without tangible rewards, much the same as life in general. Dealing with hazards and challenges of ascent forces us to focus and forget other cares. Doing this successfully is incredibly rewarding—and the victory is all yours.

Your life is really one big mountain, one that makes Mount Everest look like an anthill. So get your climbing gear and grab your pack—we're going climbing. I look forward to taking this journey with you, your personal mountain guide, as we boldly ascend the mountains of life together.

| The First Lesson |

CHOOSE YOUR MOUNTAIN

"I have my most intense feelings of existance only when,

through strain and most extreme exertion, I achieve

the bounds of human possibility, and attempt

to push these bounds still further."

—REINHOLD MESSNER, *THE WORLD'S GREATEST MOUNTAINEER*

The wind roared past me like a locomotive, tearing at my freezing body. I didn't know if this howling blizzard would last six hours or six days, and I didn't know how much longer I could hang on. I risked frostbite every time I took off my glove to wipe the icy snow from my goggles and headlamp, hoping the tiny beam from the lamp would pierce the blinding snowstorm and show me the way to safety. I had been on the move for more than twenty hours when the realization hit me: I was going to die. I had no food, no water, no oxygen; only a rib-breaking cough. I was lost and alone on Mount Everest at 26,000 feet, trying to get to Camp Four in the worst storm I had ever seen. I was mentally and physically exhausted, and desperately needed to rest, but sitting down meant risking that I would never get back up. In the dark and the snow I couldn't see where I needed to go, and I was losing the willpower to keep moving. I put my head in my hands and whispered, "God, help me. I don't know where to go." I was living my dream—finally on Mount Everest, proud to be part of the American Expedition team—yet wondering whether I would make it out alive.

∽

When I was six years old I discovered that mountains would be my destiny. I'll never forget the sense of adventure I felt paddling across that beautiful, clear, mirror-smooth mountain lake in the Canadian Rockies with my father. Having arrived at our campsite the night before, we woke before dawn to rent a canoe and explore. We paddled away from the shore, and my father patiently answered my incessant questions as we rounded a bend and came out of the thick morning mist. My eyes were drawn upwards as the mountains came into view: my heart pounded, and suddenly I was speechless. I felt a strange mixture of peace and excitement deep inside. The peaks were majestic and incredibly magnetic; the experience was larger than life. I listened intently as my father told me what he knew about mountains, and then I announced, "I want to be a mountain climber."

Two years later, in my native Australia, I learned that Mount Everest was the world's highest mountain, and it became my goal to climb it. Some people know at an early age that they want to learn to fly a plane, play music, be a school-teacher or doctor, or go to the moon. I knew I wanted to climb mountains and I knew the ultimate goal was Everest, the biggest of them all. I had found my life's purpose, and I was hungry to find out what I needed to learn to achieve that dream.

Back then I never thought about *how* I'd climb Everest. When Italian mountaineer Reinhold Messner silenced the skeptics and climbed it without supplemental oxygen in 1978, a new standard was set for mountaineers. Accomplishing a feat that most people thought was impossible, Messner threw out the challenge to climb big mountains by what he called "fair means"—without carrying extra oxygen. Messner's feat became my standard. I would climb Everest by fair means, too.

When I learned of Messner's fantastic achievement I hadn't started climbing real mountains yet. But I already believed in a similar philosophy of "clean climbing," climbing without damaging the rock by the traditional method of banging metal stakes (called pitons or bolts) into it. From the beginning, part of the attraction of climbing for me has been the chance to enjoy nature as I find it. Even at that young age, I believed that people should rise to the standard of nature, not bring things down to a lesser level just to satisfy our egos—and that the achievement and pleasure of climbing a rock face should not come at the expense of damaging or permanently scarring it. I wanted to accomplish my goals by clean climbing—otherwise I would be cheating myself (and I would know it, even if no one else did). So it was easy for me to adopt Messner's philosophy, since I was already following it in my own style of climbing. I knew that when the day came for me to tackle Everest's 29,035 feet, I wouldn't want to put on an oxygen tank. I respect everyone who climbs Everest, with or without bottled oxygen, but I wanted to see how I would do against Everest without such aids.

Standards change, and what seemed impossible yesterday will become commonplace tomorrow. In 1980, Messner climbed Everest for a second time but this time alone in three days, and in 1988 the Frenchman Marc Batard climbed it in an incredible twenty-two hours from base camp, achieving the first one-day ascent of Everest. The bar kept rising, and my goals rose with it. I had learned through rock climbing that I would push myself much harder and be far more motivated to train for something if I wasn't completely sure I could do it. The challenge, excitement, and adventure came from attempting things I didn't know whether I could do. I wanted to face my greatest fear head on, on the world's greatest mountain, on my terms.

So, my vision changed again to meet the new standard. I wanted to climb Everest alone and in one day, a feat that only three or four mountaineers in the world had accomplished. I realized that it might be impossible for me to climb that high or that fast without oxygen, but I wanted to climb it purely by my own effort or not at all. I wasn't sure if I could do it, but that motivated me all the more. The excitement lay in reaching beyond my perceived limits, in not settling for goals that I knew I could achieve. I wanted to work with nature, not against it, to reach the summit and my own highest points. In the end, it would not be the mountain that I conquered; I might stand on its summit for a brief moment, but my achievement would be conquering my own doubts and fears.

⌣

Obviously, you needn't be driven to climb an actual mountain to have a great goal for your life. However, each of us has a "mountain" we need to climb, a challenge we need to undertake. The value of pursuing a personal challenge goes far beyond the challenge itself; the pursuit helps to define you as a person, and gives shape to many aspects of your life. In this way, Messner's "fair means" philosophy helped me to develop a larger philosophy of my own, and caused me to set higher standards in all areas of my life. I consciously avoid using supports that I feel would diminish my experience in my business practices, just as I do when climbing. For example, some sales people will use any means necessary—even stretching the truth—to make a sale; back when I was in sales, being honest and fair was always more important.

Success is the result of a series of small decisions that climax in a major goal or accomplishment. Following your heart, and putting your dreams into action, are the keys to success. Ask yourself: If you could drop everything, today, and have no restrictions of time, money, or ability, what would you most love to do? It might be finally going after a law degree, running a marathon, starting your own business, or mending a close relationship. Don't think in terms of "If only I had..." but rather, "I could..." Discover or reawaken those desires that energize and excite you, explore ideas that have lain dormant deep within your most authentic self.

In the first part of this exercise, as you consider the roads to take that will lead to greater feelings of fulfillment, remember to listen only to *your* inner voice. Don't evaluate your desires in relation to other people or their reactions to your plans. Naturally, practical considerations will come into play, but to find your motivation you must first tap into the source of your inspiration—and that's an individual thing. Likewise be wary of desires that arise from the wish to be admired, or from jealousy. One person's accomplishments do not diminish those of another—we all have our own abilities and ambitions. People often don't see the value of others' goals because their own needs are so different. Your dreams may not appear glamorous, but if they are important to you, then they become great. It's the mountain that challenges and motivates you— and the standards *you* set for yourself—that are important. A worthy goal is something that will bring you deep personal satisfaction. Try to find something that is tough enough to challenge and excite you, but not so tough that it discourages you.

The road ahead may seem more challenging than anything you have ever attempted, and may even seem impossible. You may worry that the way will be difficult, painful, frightening, dangerous—perhaps even life threatening. None of that matters. How you ultimately feel about yourself is the only important thing. If you think about the people you know who go after their hearts' desires, you'll notice that they usually have an infectious lust for life, a focused purpose behind every decision they make. They know that each action is taking them closer to their goal. The combination of motivation, purpose, and progress makes for an exciting daily existence.

Knowing what it is that you want is the first step to making it a reality. You may need courage to be really honest and to allow yourself to articulate your dream. But consider the payoff: life is more meaningful, and more fun, when you awaken every day to the possibility of fulfilling your dreams. Choosing a mountain to climb is tremendously satisfying, especially once you begin to cast your doubts and fears aside and break through the obstacles in your way. Going for your personal summit creates an energy that radiates into everything you do, and touches everyone with whom you come into contact. You can't always control external forces, and you can't always determine the outcome of your efforts, but you can always make your best attempt, give your dream your best shot; that is what's important.

Choosing your mountain—the goal or dream that really excites and challenges you—is the first step toward a more fulfilling life. Making the decision to go for it can be the most difficult part. However, just taking this first step in the direction of your mountain will give you the confidence and motivation to take another step, and then another. Each step moves you closer to your personal summit. The strength you will gain from simply trying will make you bolder in every area of your life. This can translate into asking for that date, requesting that raise, or making that move to a new place. You will experience setbacks, fear, and doubt, but now you'll know they needn't hold you back. Your summit, your mountaintop, is within reach. Go for it!

Steps to choosing your mountain:

- Take the time to think about what you'd really like to accomplish in your life. (Stay true to yourself, and don't be concerned with what others might think.)

- Sit down and write out exactly what you would do if you could drop everything today, and you had no restrictions of time, money, or ability.

- Now consider, with your current situation, what your realistic short and long-term goals could be. (Know that you will have setbacks—regardless, you will give it your best shot.)

- When you've made your choice, celebrate it!

The Second Lesson

MASTER YOUR SKILLS

Mountains are the most powerful places on earth,

and demand the utmost respect.

—Erik Weihenmayer, *the first blind mountaineer*

to climb Mount Everest

*O*ne spring day in 1990, I grabbed my mail on the way out the door. One letter caught my eye: an official-looking envelope that bore a blue logo, "1991 American Everest Expedition." I'm sure I was shaking as I read the words from our expedition leader:

> Dear Gary:
>
> It is with great pleasure that we invite you to join the 1991 American Everest Expedition. We all feel that you will be a strong addition to our highly skilled team. We look forward to sharing this once-in-a-lifetime experience with you. . . .

After twenty-five years of preparation, I was going to Everest! To stand on Everest's summit is to reach the earth's apex, and to know that no one can journey higher by his or her own power. Here was my chance to achieve my ultimate dream, my destiny. I'd spent much of my life pushing my limits on peaks around the world, developing the skills and gaining the experience necessary for Everest, always carrying the vision of testing myself on earth's highest mountain. In one year, I would get the chance to attempt my ultimate goal.

⌐

When I was nine years old we moved to Canberra, Australia's capital, near a beautiful wilderness area called the Brindabella Mountains. They could hardly be considered mountains by world standards, but they did get snow in the winter, and they proved to be a fantastic training ground for my first few years in the hills. Fortunately for me, we lived on the outskirts of town, and I started my mountain apprenticeship by going on day hikes close to home. I graduated to "bushwalking" trips, as hiking is called in Australia (because there are very few trails, and very thick undergrowth). As my friends and I got braver over the next year, and our parents less worried about us surviving in the bush, we ventured on longer and harder overnight trips.

After a few easier trips, my friends, Marc and Peter, and I all thought we were ready to tackle our first "mountain." My father dropped us off early one Saturday morning at the end of the dirt road, about fifty miles south of Canberra. Since there were absolutely no trails, we headed straight into the bush, totally dependent on our map and compass. Our goal was to climb the 6,124-foot Tidbinbilla Peak, one of the highest peaks in the Brindabella range.

We spent several hours battling through the thick bush, stopping for lunch right at the base of the peak. Six hours later, after struggling up the near-vertical undergrowth with our packs, we sat down to rest. Then the wind picked up, it started to rain, and nightfall was almost upon us. We needed to find a place to pitch our small tent and to dry out, but there was nowhere flat enough to set it up. We were wet, cold, and tired, but we had to press on. We reached the top of the peak's narrow ridge and pulled out our only flashlight. Marc took it and carefully crept along the ridge, looking for a place to camp so that we could get out of the cold, driving rain. Marc yelled that he had found a place, and Peter and I charged into the wind to find him. The spot was small and rocky, but we were so tired from fighting the storm that we had to make do with it. We struggled to put up the tent in the wind as we discussed our situation. We had no water left, so our next problem was how to soothe our parched throats. We rigged a funnel and gathered enough water to drink and to make hot soup on our small butane stove. Cooking inside the cramped tent was difficult, but we made light of our situation and told jokes to break the tension.

As we finished dinner, the storm intensified. On this exposed ridge we were sitting ducks for lightning strikes, but we didn't know what else we could do. The wind was so strong that we worried the whole tent would take off, especially since it didn't have a sewn-in floor. Sitting on a tarp we'd placed under the tent, each of us held down as much of the tent as we could grab. The storm swirled all around us and we cringed with each lightning strike and thunderclap. We were dead tired—especially after hanging onto the tent for dear life for several hours—but with the stress of the storm none of us could sleep until well past midnight, when the thunder and lightning stopped and the wind died down. The rain continued relentlessly.

As the next day dawned, I woke first, and I had to laugh when I saw how Marc and Peter had fallen asleep, desperately clutching the sides of the tent. We were all soaked to the skin, but luckily it looked like it would be a nice day and we'd have a chance to dry out. We *all* laughed when we saw the precarious ridge we were on. Had we known it was that steep right outside our tent, we probably would have been too frightened to sleep at all. We slapped each others' backs, feeling very happy to have survived the night. After a soggy breakfast we climbed the hundred or so feet to the tiny rocky summit of Tidbinbilla Peak. The sky was clear and we could see for miles in every direction. The beauty and the magnificence of the view took my breath away. I had just spent the most uncomfortable—and certainly most frightening—night of my life, but once I saw that incredible view, all the pain and suffering evaporated and I knew that it had been worth it. This was my first real mountain, and I was hooked.

Along with the exhilaration of that experience came a greater respect for nature. We had been lucky, but there isn't much room for luck when exposed to the elements. The Sherpas (the best known of the mountain tribes of Nepal, famous for their hard work on Himalayan expeditions) believe that you will have safe passage if you climb in a way that honors the mountains. To put in your time gaining the skills, and preparing for whatever weather or conditions the mountain hands out, shows your respect. Climbing only to satisfy one's ego, and without the necessary skill and experience, is not honoring the mountains, and the Sherpas believe such actions may be punished. No one conquers a mountain, but the mountain may allow you, if you deserve it, to stand for a moment on its summit.

Once I really started studying mountain climbing, it was obvious that becoming accomplished in this activity would require a significant amount of effort. Some dreams require more physical exertion and training, while for others the preparation is more mental. Some people are natural at pursuing their dream and improvement comes quickly and easily to them. Others, like me, have to struggle and work hard for every inch. But I was willing to put in the time and effort.

I also learned that I'd need very specific equipment, so I started reading magazines and catalogs to learn about the different types of gear. I window-shopped at hiking and climbing stores, weighing the merits of the enticing displays. I stopped spending my pocket money on candy and other boyish items, and saved up for a much-needed sleeping bag and backpack. I'd been using my father's heavy and uncomfortable army pack, and *his* father's World War II sleeping bag, which was so worn that it was practically useless.

At age eleven, after many great adventures and thousands of miles walking in the bush (which helped me develop great navigational and survival skills), I knew that it was time to move to the next level. To continue my climbing "studies," I saved more pocket money for months to buy a real climbing rope, read more climbing books, and then recruited Marc— my bushwalking buddy—to go rock climbing for the very first time. We went to a small fifty-foot-high rock quarry not far from our boarding school. Climbing this relatively simple rock face was the most frightening and difficult thing I had ever done. But even after that first, scary attempt, I couldn't wait to go back.

From that first experience it was obvious how dangerous climbing was, and how important it was to do things the right way. The consequences of making the wrong decision could be tragic. So I spent my time studying climbing—to the point where my school grades suffered, though I would have received an A+ in climbing. I joined the school outdoor club and tagged along every time they went rock climbing. Though rock climbing never came easily to me, my knowledge of what to do and not to do grew quickly. Simon Parker, a school buddy, became my regular climbing partner. As soon as the final bell rang on Friday, we would pick up our food from the boardinghouse kitchen, race back to the dorm, change clothes, grab our packs, and start walking the five miles to the road that headed out of town.

The closest real rock climbing area was called Booroomba Rocks, a remote, six-hundred-foot granite cliff. It was fifty miles from the school, and we'd try to hitchhike all the way there, but would usually end up hiking the last few miles to the climbers' campsite, arriving exhausted around midnight.

Regardless of what time we got to bed, we'd get up early and climb all day until it got dark, do the same on Sunday, then try to get a ride with a climber who was driving back to town. If we couldn't find a ride it would be another long hike back to the main road and a hitchhike back to school, where we'd get the third degree about being so late. (Much later I realized how amazing it was that the school even let us go. Part of that is probably due to the adventurous Australian spirit. No doubt our teachers also saw our commitment to climbing, and thought it better for us to be running wild in the wilderness than in town.)

One weekend at the end of the climbing season we were late reaching our campsite at the top of the cliff. We were not prepared for the snow that started early the next morning. I had not even taken a sleeping bag, preferring to carry less weight. That was the last time I would make that mistake. After a cold night, we started the long hike back to the main road. Back then I thought that a wet weekend was a waste of time, but now I realize how much those experiences taught me about being better prepared, and how they shaped my character and mental toughness. Today, I am far better able to deal both mentally and physically with adverse conditions, in my work, in my personal life, and in the outdoors—and I know what to bring and not to bring on a trip. Mastering skills comes from putting in the miles, from getting out there and doing it.

Erik Weihenmayer, the blind mountaineer who climbed Everest in 2001, came under criticism for supposedly putting his partners at risk in pursuit of his own goals. I was pleasantly surprised when his climbing partners said they would rather climb with Erik than with many sighted climbers. They knew that Erik had spent so much time learning his skills that he was a safe and skilled mountaineer. Erik had spent endless hours handling each piece of equipment till he knew it inside and out, better than people with ten times as many years in the mountains. He understood that he had a sight limitation, but he overcame it by spending a great deal of time in the mountains so he would have more than enough experience for the ascent. He probably wouldn't have found a team to climb with if he had not mastered his skills.

Early on, I read that it took fifteen to twenty years of climbing before you were ready to go to the Himalayas with any degree of safety, so I took my time and worked through easier climbs, then more difficult ones, mastering each level before moving onto the next. I focused on what I needed to do on a daily basis, not on my final goal. It takes hundreds of days in the mountains to learn how to climb safely on the different types of rock, snow, and ice, and to learn about weather, geology, navigation, winter survival, first aid, communication, teamwork, mountain hazards, altitude, nutrition, hydration, physical conditioning, equipment, and gear packing—let alone to develop your own instinctive skills. I started with hiking and rock climbing before moving onto snow and ice climbing, and I knew that each skill would build upon the previous. I built a strong foundation that has served me well in my mountaineering career. I learned something important from every mile I hiked, every climb I attempted, and every rain- or snowstorm I endured.

I understood that I would have to do two things to be a mountain climber. First, I had to learn all the skills necessary to be prepared for the mountains I wanted to climb; second, I had to start small and work my way up. I knew that paying my dues early on would benefit me greatly in the long run. Sadly, I've lost many friends in the mountains; one reason that I'm still around is the tremendous amount of time I have put into mastering my skills. Whenever I met other climbers, I would pick their brains for ways to improve. I knew that I could learn from different outlooks, perspectives, and techniques. Some of these climbers became good friends, and their interest in my development was another source of support and insight.

The breadth and depth of the experience you have acquired should determine the size and scale of your next challenge. Mastering the skills required to succeed on your mountain will allow you to be better prepared and make fewer mistakes. This in turn will give you the confidence and ability to go higher. As you gain more skills and experience, your potential will increase. Young climbers often want to jump straight to the harder climbs, though they have trouble with simple climbing techniques. Because they haven't mastered the foundational skills, those relatively "easy" moves are far more difficult than they should be, and therefore the climb is harder and more dangerous. It's the same whether you are trying to run a company, write a book, or cook a great meal. If you don't know the basics, the result is usually disappointing. When you cut corners, you miss the basic foundational skills. Without the proper foundation, even apparent competence will be shaky and fall apart the first time you confront a problem or impasse. As the saying goes, there are no shortcuts to success.

Being out in all types of weather also prepares you for tough times in the mountains. I thrive on climbing in bad weather, as I know it is great training for the bad weather that is typical high in the Himalayas. The preparations of those experiences saved my life (and the lives of those with me) more than once. Don't cancel your plans because of obstacles; go out and gain experience from them. You will learn more from the hard times than from the easy times, and you can achieve almost anything if you are willing to put the time and effort into the foundation.

Finally, respect the mountain. Allow yourself to be humbled—though not daunted—by the vast amount you still don't know about your new field of pursuit. Be conservative in your estimates of the time and energy needed to reach your goal, and know that the more time you spend in preparation, the less effort will be required. Spending time sharpening an axe before you cut down a tree is hard, boring work, but it will allow you to cut down the tree in far less time, and with much less effort.

Steps to mastering your skills:

- Identify the skills that you will need to master in order to accomplish your goal.
- Determine what smaller goals will get you closer to your larger goal.
- Allocate the time necessary to achieve your objective.
- Focus on whatever needs to be done.
- Be patient. Put in the time, and know you will be rewarded.
- Find mentors who are willing to help you.
- Accept that nothing great comes easily or quickly.
- Use unexpected obstacles to sharpen your skills.
- Respect your mountain.

The Third Lesson

LIGHTEN YOUR LOAD

If you take bivouac equipment along, you will bivouac.

—YVON CHOUINARD, CLIMBER, PHILOSOPHER, AND
FOUNDER OF PATAGONIA EQUIPMENT

I couldn't sleep that night after getting the invitation. I woke early and worked out with a renewed intensity. I would have to be in the best shape of my life to climb Everest, let alone to climb it without supplementary oxygen (or "O's"). At the time, only about thirty other climbers had achieved non-oxygen ascents, but my goal was even more ambitious. I wanted to climb it in less than twenty-four hours. At that time, only one person, Frenchman Marc Batard—Le sprinter de L'Everest—had done so.

My physical and mental preparation was intense. At the time I was living in Colorado Springs, Colorado, home of the United States Olympic Training Center and located 6,000 feet above sea level. The sports trainers there generously directed my workouts, which was a tremendous benefit. I had 14,110-foot Pikes Peak in my backyard, the trailhead only twenty minutes' drive from my home. Through that winter, I hiked the 8,000-foot elevation gain and twenty-six-mile round trip twice a week, which formed the cornerstone of my training (that equaled two hard, high-altitude marathons a week—with a thirty-pound pack). Additional running, weight training, stretching, and intense psychological feedback sessions rounded out my regime. Training, seeking equipment sponsors, organizing a support trek into Everest base

camp for eighteen friends, and my blossoming rela-
tionship with my future wife, on top of my full-time
job, left little time for sleep or anything else. The days
flew by. It was almost time.

࿔

There came a day when I'd had enough of technical rock climbing. At the time, I was in top form and had been climbing six days a week for about three years. Midway through a ten-day climbing trip to a cliff in northeastern Australia, right at the top of a very challenging rock climb, I knew that I was done. As I packed to go home that night, to my climbing partner Simon's dismay, I tried to explain the revelation that my true calling was mountaineering, climbing big snow- and ice-covered mountains, like those in the Himalayas. Rock climbing had been a way of gaining the experience I needed to tackle big mountains—a means to an end—but for Simon, rock climbing was his life. I was bored with focusing all my energy on a piece of rock inches from my nose, and I needed to move on. I hitchhiked the two thousand miles back to Adelaide, sold practically everything I owned, bought a motorcycle, and rode it to Sydney. I worked two jobs and saved every cent I could, with the goal of traveling overseas for the challenge of climbing some *real* mountains.

"I'll see you in a few years," I said as I grabbed my small daypack, which contained everything I owned, and pulled out my one-way ticket. As I turned to wave one last time to the group that had come to see me off, the magnitude of what I was doing hit me. I was leaving everything I was familiar with—my friends, my life, the beach, and the city of Sydney that I loved. It was 1982 and I had just turned twenty-four. I was both fearful and excited. Was I doing the right thing? Was this responsible? What did my parents think? Was I nuts for leaving? I was tempted to turn around and say I'd changed my mind, that traveling and climbing in the Himalayas wasn't really that important. But I needed to leave. I needed an adventure. I needed to put my life back on the edge. I smiled, turned, and walked briskly onto the plane.

The sun was just coming up when we landed, and it was already stifling hot as I walked across the melting blacktop to the terminal of the Calcutta International Airport. The intense heat made India less appealing, even for an Aussie like me who was used to hot weather. The airport was wretchedly hot, humid, and teeming with people—who, I learned, came to the airport for something to do. I found a bus heading downtown. As I stared out the window at the filthy sidewalks and streets, the dust and smoke in the air, the throngs of people, and the scrawny dogs and cows wandering through the haphazard, congested traffic, I secretly wished the bus would keep going and deliver me from this uncomfortable and foreign place. I now regretted my decision to fly here and travel overland to the Himalayas to save some of my hard-earned money.

After a few days in Calcutta I was more than ready to leave the squalor and heat behind, and head for the higher and cooler terrain of Darjeeling, on my way to Nepal and the Himalayas. From the quaint town of Darjeeling there is an incredible view of Mount Kangchenjunga, the third highest mountain in the world, standing at 28,750 feet. It was over a hundred miles away but it was enormous, almost beyond belief. Seeing it rekindled my desire to climb Everest, yet at the same time the scale of it intimidated me. Two days later, after a very long jeep ride on which everything that could possibly go wrong did, I arrived in the medieval city of Kathmandu, Nepal, and I felt like I'd come home. I ended up living in Nepal and working as a guide. Even though it was still years before I would tackle Everest itself, this was the beginning of my Himalayan climbing career.

The small daypack I had brought from Australia held a tiny, two-pound sleeping bag, a camera, a few rolls of film, a few bathroom items, a hand towel, a small knife, a pair of shorts, a spare T-shirt, and a spare pair of socks. That was all I had, except for my passport and traveler's checks in a waist belt, and the clothes on my back, for a few years' traveling. If it got cold I would buy a sweater. I would get climbing equipment and clothing wherever I was and would learn how to use "foreign" gear. I wanted to experience everything anew and gain a fresh perspective. Uncluttered with the past, I was open to experiencing the future and new horizons.

Long hikes with heavy packs through the dense Australian bush to remote cliffs had convinced me that there had to be a smarter way to travel, so I had discovered the tremendous advantages of traveling light. I started to experiment, to learn what I needed and what I could do without. I learned to rely on my own ability, rather than carrying my courage in my pack (by bringing equipment and extra clothing "just in case I needed it"—which I rarely did). Going as light as possible made climbing more fun, and got me closer to the adventure I sought through climbing in the first place.

I was traveling light on this trip in many ways beyond my luggage. I had left Australia with no debt, no bills, no house, no car, no bank account—I didn't even own a watch. I didn't owe anything to anybody, had no place I had to be, no job, no schedule, no responsibilities, and no ticket home. I had money, spare clothes, a passport, an open mind, and a desire to see the Himalayas and learn new things. I'm thankful that I made the decision to leave behind the "securities" of life, which it is so easy to believe are important.

When I take people climbing for the first time, they usually pack far too much equipment for the trip. They are worried they "might need this . . . or that," which often boils down to a lack of confidence in their ability. Some people spend their entire trip packing and unpacking, searching for things in a cluttered and overstuffed backpack or travel bag. They also suffer pain and exhaustion from carrying a heavier than necessary pack. The less you take, the more you learn how little you need. Travel to the third world and you'll begin to appreciate how little others have, and how happy and content they are without all the material possessions we think we can't leave behind. If you carry too much equipment you will reach fewer summits—that's guaranteed. World-class mountaineers become world-class because they don't carry extra gear. They learn to travel light. They rely on their own skill, experience, and judgment, not on the gear sitting in their packs.

Many climbers will blame a failed climb on feeling sick or tired, sleeping badly, not being acclimated, or getting caught in a storm, when all of those problems were actually symptoms of carrying too much weight. In the mountains, climbing is far safer when you can move quickly and easily, so traveling light reduces your exposure to the elements and other potential dangers.

I have a rule that I follow when I organize my gear for a climb; I call it the 50/50 rule. Shortly before a climb, I spread out everything I "need." I take my time, over a few days, to look over the gear, and to think through each part of the climb, making sure that I have all the equipment and clothing that I will need for a safe and successful ascent and descent. I then gather all the gear I know that I will *definitely* use, making sure that every item will play an important role or a key emergency function, setting everything else aside. I also make sure that I'm not doubling up on what my climbing partner is taking, and discuss what items we can share. Then comes the fun part. My goal is to pack about half of the pile that's left. That leaves me with a twenty-five- to thirty-five-pound pack for a two- to four-day climbing trip—about half of what most people carry!

Often, it's the extra items that people throw into their packs at the last minute that lower their chance of success on climbs. The trick is to keep focusing on the goal: to safely climb a mountain, and to have fun! It's difficult to have fun if you have sore shoulders at the end of the day, and it's hard to be safe when you are caught out in a storm because you were slowed down by a pack full of things you don't need. The same is true in daily life. Focus on your goal; don't miss out on achieving it because of being encumbered with items that you'll never need or use.

I taught ice climbing professionally for three winters, six days a week, with a ten-year-old ice hammer that I bought in a gear shop in Kathmandu for $20. I climbed Mount McKinley, one of the world's coldest mountains, alone, in a pair of Gore-Tex running pants that I bought for $10 in a garage sale. You can buy the latest skis every year, or buy skis every third year and use the money you save to ski in New Zealand. The improvement in your skiing ability with new skis will be outweighed by the experience and skills you gain by skiing in a different county, not to mention the wonderful memories you will have. Traveling light means not feeling the need to buy the latest and greatest gear all the time, which will only detract from your reliance on your own ability and skill. (The exception: upgrading gear to make it weigh less—now *that's* worth the money!)

With fewer things, you pack more quickly; find things faster; have less to lose, break, or get stolen; have less to worry about; will spend less; and, more importantly, have less clutter to interrupt the real purpose of your trip. Learn to place more faith in yourself than in the gear you carry. When you get back from a trip or finish a project, review your equipment, and learn from what you didn't use. Rarely will you find that you didn't have enough with you.

Spending your time getting rid of possessions, rather than buying more, is the key to simplifying life. This includes piles of papers, projects you never get to, and might-come-in-handy-someday supplies crammed in your garage, attic, and closets. Clutter not only fills your physical environment but also your brain, slowing you down, distracting you, and making it difficult to accomplish your real goals. Most people go on holiday with far too much luggage, and go through life with far too much baggage. Leave behind the things that will weigh you down, and that take your focus off your goals and dreams. Make room for more of what you really need. A weekend or month spent getting rid of the extraneous "stuff" that you have accumulated will be well worth the time. Ask yourself why you hold on to things, and try to whittle your possessions down to only those things you actually use. If you have clothes, tools, equipment you haven't used in over a year (or at the most, two years), get rid of them. Letting go of belongings releases a power, and creates a vacuum that forces the universe to fill the void. If we took the time to notice, we'd see that whatever we *truly* need is provided for us.

Our consumer society is constantly selling us possessions, quite successfully conditioning people to believe that they always need more things to have a fulfilling life. The irony is that traveling through life with so much stuff often *prevents* people from experiencing life. They miss half the adventure, insulating themselves from risk or adversity by hiding behind their belongings. Freeing yourself of the belief that you always need more possessions can also lead to greater satisfaction with what you have. Over time, as you wean yourself from your dependency on things, and place more faith in your abilities, you'll carry fewer "backup" items. It is as simple as that. The bottom line: pack less, learn (through experience) what you can do without, and enjoy increased energy and success in all areas of your life—particularly when facing new challenges.

Steps to lightening your load:

- Master your skills; be wary of carrying equipment to make up for a lack of skills.
- Remove the clutter from your life: from your car, home, office—and backpack.

- When you finish a trip, or any other activity, be sure to look at what you did and didn't use, and learn from that.

- Keep your life simple. Realize that less is more, in all areas of your life.

- Know that your true security comes from within, not from what you carry.

The Fourth Lesson

BELIEVE IN YOURSELF

Assume a virtue, if you have it not.

—Shakespeare

*T*he 1991 American Everest Expedition team met in early March in Kathmandu, the capital of Nepal. After a couple of days getting the necessary permits, packing our equipment, and buying food, we were ready to head for the mountains. Early one morning we flew by small plane to Lukla airstrip, at 9,000 feet, to begin our two-week trek to Everest's base camp. The rocky base camp at 17,500 feet was reached after a long, hard day crossing the Khumbu Glacier, which descends from the infamous Khumbu Icefall and the higher flanks of Everest.

We spent a week getting acclimatized while we set up our camp, organized our loads for going higher on the mountain, and waited for a Buddhist Lama to arrive from Pangboche Monastery, three days' walk away. The Lama finally arrived and performed the traditional half-day ceremony that precedes anyone setting foot on the mountain. With eight climbers on our team, and knowing the odds that one in ten won't return from a Himalayan expedition, everyone said some form of prayer during the ceremony, regardless of their beliefs. The next morning we began carrying supplies through the treacherous Khumbu Icefall, an ever-changing field of ice with seemingly bottomless crevasses and huge blocks of ice ready to collapse at any moment. It was dangerous and exhausting, but

> *unavoidable, because we needed to supply our higher*
> *camps with provisions for the ascent.*

∽

Most of us know that it's important to believe in ourselves—or so we've been told at some point in our lives. For the idea to take on real meaning, however, it needs to be connected to something that illustrates its power. I can't think of a better way to prove this point than telling Gary Guller's story. British by birth, Gary started rock climbing at the age of thirteen, in the United States. From his first experience, he climbed every chance he had. In winter he would hitchhike from his home in North Carolina to ice climb in New Hampshire, and in summer he'd head west to California and Washington, looking for higher mountains and more difficult routes. While in high school he climbed every weekend on nearby cliffs, those weekends often turning into weeks, much to his parents' and teachers' concern. After graduating, he lived life to the fullest—young, free, single, not a worry in the world, doing what he loved to do. He worked as a climbing instructor, and did whatever he could to earn money to get to the next mountain. Gary believed that nothing could or would ever happen to him, that he was invincible.

He soon set his sights on the bigger mountains of the world, and at the age of twenty-one Gary arranged his first international climbing expedition, to the volcanoes in Mexico. With him was his best friend and longtime climbing partner, Jerry, and their goal was to climb a new route on the 18,880-foot Pico De Orizaba, Mexico's highest mountain. Three weeks later, however, Jerry was dead, and Gary was being evacuated back to the United States. They had been close to the summit, and the ice was steep and hard as glass, barely allowing their crampons to bite. The wind picked up and blew Jerry off the face. Roped together, Gary and Jerry fell more than 1,500 feet before they stopped just short of a large crevasse. Three days later the rescue team arrived, carrying two body bags. Gary was in such excruciating pain, and so close to death, that he felt like crawling into the second bag.

Gary's neck was broken in two places, fractured in a third. The nerves in his spine were damaged so badly that his left arm was completely paralyzed. Despite experimental surgery to regain movement of his arm, the paralysis was irreparable. Two years in and out of hospitals, umpteen operations, intolerable pain, and the very real possibility of not being able to climb again were almost too much for him. Climbing meant everything to Gary, and having one arm that was useless only reminded him of his inability to climb. To a mountaineer this was beyond comprehension. Gary often thought of suicide, believing his life was essentially over.

Gary made the difficult decision to have his arm amputated. He thought that not clinging to the hope that he might recover the use of his arm would free him of the memory of what had happened—of the accident, of those three horrible days waiting to die, of the best friend he had lost, of the carefree life that seemed to be gone forever. But it didn't work. Chronic pain, and mental anguish and embarrassment (at having one arm, and not being able to do more than easy hikes) made him angry and bitter. He retreated from his friends and family. An addiction to painkillers led to deep depression, which soon led to hard drinking and hard drugs. This was by far the toughest and most dangerous mountain he had ever been on, and there didn't seem to be a way to get off.

Gary woke one morning on a pillow soaked with blood after a night of heavy cocaine use. Scared, he knew he needed to make a change or die. His mountaintop would no longer be the hard liquor or the white powder he craved. He decided to make something of his life before he destroyed it. He hit the road, not heading anywhere in particular, wanting only to sober up and clear his mind. He needed to think, and to search his inner being for what was left. He would drive all night, then hike up an easy mountain. He stopped thinking about what he couldn't do and started thinking about what he could do. He started to think about the mountains he could climb. Gary Guller started to dream again.

And he started climbing even tougher and higher mountains within himself:

The mountain of self-consciousness.

The mountain of doubt.

The mountain of insecurity.

The mountain of addiction.

The mountain of fear.

And he thought hard about the questions that had plagued him every moment since the accident:

Will I ever marry?

Will I be accepted again?

Will I ever have friends again?

Will I ever climb again?

Am I still a man?

Am I still a person?

Can I keep myself sober and drug free?

Can I forgive myself for how low I let myself go?

Gary decided that even though it sounded simplistic and idealistic, anything was possible for him if he changed his thinking and started to believe in himself. Even though all the doctors had told him that he'd never climb again, and society looked at him as handicapped, his war cry became, "Anything Is Possible!" Gary decided to shout, "Yes I can!" back at the doubters, and to show them what he could do. He let himself believe he had the right to be successful, happy, and free to live his life the way he wanted, and that his potential and his future were boundless.

Regaining confidence and strength, Gary climbed peaks in Europe and South America. He spent time trekking and climbing in Nepal, and met Joni on the trail in the Himalayas. They married, and started their own adventure travel business in Nepal. Fourteen years after his accident, with the support of his wife and family and a large group of friends, Gary organized and led the "Anything Is Possible Mount Everest Expedition," on which two members reached the summit. The goals of the expedition were to raise awareness and support for people with disabilities, and demonstrate that their lives and dreams are as important as anyone else's. Not long after, I joined Gary Guller as the co-leader of Team Everest '03, where he became the first person with one arm to climb Mount Everest.

Believing in yourself, obviously, is a mental process. Gary woke up one day and decided to change his life. Physically he was no different; he still had only one arm, but he changed the record playing in his head. He accepted himself as he was, and decided to move forward with his life and not dwell in the past. He made the choice to put a smile on his face and to focus on what he could do, not on what he couldn't. He made the choice to forgive himself for whatever he didn't like about his past. He started looking at what his life could be. Gary Guller had sunk about as low as you can go, yet he made the decision to change, to accept himself as he was. Did he have moments of doubt? Absolutely. Did he have setbacks? Certainly. But whenever that happened he pulled himself together, moved on, and forgave himself, just like you and I must do if we want to live the life we are meant to live.

You may not be able to transform your thought process overnight as Gary did, but you can take small steps to get there. For example, there was a point in my adult life when I was very insecure and self-conscious, and had little confidence in social and business situations. One day I read a quote by William Shakespeare that literally changed my life: "Assume a virtue, if you have it not." I decided to assume that I had more confidence by acting more confidently, and by doing so I somehow convinced myself that I did have more confidence. Soon enough, I started feeling more confident, and over time I *became* more confident. Part of that transition was achieved by realizing that I had no reason to be insecure about myself, no reason *not* to be confident. Many people live in fear, and are insecure and awkward in social situations. They could change their lives if they applied this method. Actors assume different virtues all the time, so why shouldn't a salesperson or a guest at a party assume more confidence? I have found that actions are rewarded with feedback, both positive and negative. Be willing to try and to fail; that's how you will learn and gain more confidence and belief in yourself. But also be willing to succeed.

Recently, a friend asked me to wish her luck because she had an interview for a job the next day. I asked her if she felt that she deserved the position. Confused, she asked me what that had to do with anything. I replied that she would certainly stand out from the dozens of other applicants if she walked into the interview confident in herself and believing that she deserved the job. Why should an employer hire her if she didn't believe that she would be an excellent choice for the position? Act like the person you want to become. If you can't believe that you deserve to reach your goals, why bother trying?

The difference between winners and losers in any field usually comes down to psychology; specifically, people's belief and confidence in themselves. When faced with a daunting task, it helps to remind yourself that you are capable of doing an excellent job. Salespeople should walk into a meeting believing that they deserve the sale. Many athletes give up mentally before they give up physically. An athlete who wants to win an Olympic Gold medal four years down the road must make *daily* decisions on how hard to train or what food to eat. A successful salesperson makes *daily* decisions to study business trends and attend seminars that will benefit them. Visualize this process as physically building a foundation of confidence and belief in yourself. Every positive thing you do adds another brick to strengthen your foundation; a negative action takes one away.

Other actions also add or take away from your foundation of confidence. For example, if you believe that smoking cigarettes, or eating donuts, or not washing your car every week is bad behavior, then every time you light up, eat a donut, or don't wash your car, you take away blocks of confidence from your foundation, essentially undermining your belief in yourself. Every time you don't do what you say you will do, you weaken your resolve and begin to build the habit of not following through. Bad habits keep you in bondage and rob you of self-confidence.

It's important to remember that while you practice confidence and cultivate your belief in your abilities, you won't automatically succeed in everything you do. There are lessons to be learned every step of the way, and often we can't see where we still need instruction until something unanticipated happens and we are left to make sense of it afterward. People who have figured this out will also use their failures as building blocks to add to their foundation, because they know that they can learn from their mistakes or lapses in judgment, and they don't take failure personally. People with a weak foundation are debilitated when things don't turn out as they expect, viewing failure as proof that they don't have what it takes.

Believing in yourself requires you to accept yourself, as you are, with all of your strengths and weaknesses. When you accept yourself you can like yourself, and when you like yourself you can love yourself, and when this happens you can truly love others and believe in yourself. My whole world changed when I made the decision to accept myself as I was—the good, the bad, and the ugly—and to simply *like* myself. Once I accepted myself, I could accept others for who they were, too, and relationships that had been strained changed dramatically for the better.

The way to not lose faith in yourself on a big mountain, or on a big project, is by knowing that in the past you have done what you said you would do on a smaller scale. You can program your body for success by working out, and program your mind for success by doing what you say you are going to do. Learn and profit from the past, but live in the present and create the life you want. Once you trust yourself you will start to believe in yourself more and more. Once you believe in yourself, your whole world will change!

Steps to believing in yourself:

- Acknowledge and accept your past for what it is, and learn from it.
- Accept yourself as you are, recognizing that you can overcome your weaknesses.
- Brick by brick, build a strong fortress of self-confidence and belief in yourself.
- Change your habits; follow through on your commitments to build your self-trust.
- Assume confidence!

The Fifth Lesson

OVERCOME YOUR FEAR

Courage is resistance to fear, mastery of fear—

not absence of fear.

—MARK TWAIN

*T*he icefall's jumble of house-sized ice blocks churns and grinds like a living train wreck for more than a mile, creating avalanches and carrying ice and snow down from the lofty basin between Everest and its neighboring peaks, Lhotse and Nuptse. Crevasses hundreds of feet deep can open or close without warning, offering icy tombs for the careless and unfortunate. So dangerous and frightening was the icefall that one team member returned home after going through it once. During the six weeks it took the team to stock the higher camps, we would climb up and down the icefall more than a dozen times. Though the fear factor diminishes after weeks of crossings, the sense of awe and constant danger never subsides. By mid-May everything was ready and in place for our attempt on the summit. Everything, that is, except my health—the debilitating chest infection and cough that I couldn't shake. Two team members had already dropped out due to illness; if things didn't improve, I would soon be the third.

⌁

I met Dave and Bruce in a climbing shop in Santa Barbara, on the southern California coast, in the spring of 1994. After a couple of months climbing together they invited me to join them on an ascent of El Capitan in Yosemite Valley, a climb they'd been planning for some time. I had first read about El Cap back in Australia when I was fourteen years old. I had stared with both excitement and trepidation at pictures of the 3,000-foot vertical granite wall that seemed impossible to climb. In those days, when I was still rock climbing, I had dreamed that some day I would get the opportunity to climb it, but with my rusty rock climbing skills the prospect of actually doing so now seemed more like a nightmare.

I had climbed many sheer rock faces and a few Himalayan peaks, but El Cap was more than three times as high, much steeper, and of a more sustained difficulty than any rock face I had yet attempted. The idea of having huge amounts of space beneath me had stopped me from trying cliffs like this before. It seemed that whenever I ascended more than 1,000 feet off the ground on a steep cliff, fear would take over and my climbing ability would crumble. On El Cap I would be experiencing nonstop fear for three or four days, far above my 1,000-foot threshold. There would be no escaping it, as we would even be sleeping on the side of its vertical face. I wondered if this climb was a smart thing to do, and worried about letting the team down if we failed on my account. Fear, I thought, was a major stumbling block, especially for someone driven to become a great climber. Regardless, I decided to rise to the challenge, and attempt the famous climb on this magnificent rock face, which I had wanted to do since childhood.

Looking up from the base of El Cap on the first morning of our climb, I felt like I was about to hop into a tiny boat and paddle across an ocean. The scale was off the charts. The overhanging wall appeared too huge to even consider climbing. We started climbing quickly, and before I knew it we'd reached a good ledge on which to stop for the night. I had survived the first day and was encouraged. Sitting with my legs dangling over the void, watching the sun drop over the horizon, I realized that we were about a thousand feet above the valley floor. Keeping my apprehensions to myself, I knew that the next day would be the real test.

Waking at dawn I lay still, attempting to postpone the day as long as possible, but all too soon it began, and after a rushed breakfast and a few hundred feet of difficult climbing, it was my turn to lead. I climbed to a tiny ledge about 150 feet higher up where, fortunately, I could rest as I surveyed the moves ahead. They were some of the most difficult on that section, though (according to our guidebook) well within my ability.

I moved my feet onto higher footholds, found a grip, small as it was, for my left hand, and tried to pull up on that while pushing with my feet. The wall was vertical, and I couldn't see or feel anything above for my right hand. I started to panic. I knew this feeling of fear well—dry mouth, sweaty brow, muscle fatigue, and an upset stomach. My mind echoed one thought: *What if I fall?*

I moved back down to the ledge and tried to calm my breathing. I wiped the sweat from my eyes with my sleeve and tried to avoid looking down but couldn't help myself. Below me was nothing but air for the height of two Empire State buildings. The warning taste of nausea hit the back of my throat. I tried moving up again and again but each time I reached the same place the fear of falling would kick in and I'd retreat back down to the ledge. I did not want to commit myself to what might, or might not, be above. What if I couldn't find any handhold and couldn't do the move? I had every reason to be scared. I also knew that the longer I dwelt on what could happen, the more I would become paralyzed by fear. I knew that it was best to clear my mind and move as quickly as possible—which is easy to reason, but hard to do. I knew the guys would be getting impatient, so I had a decision to make. I could go for it, or yell down that I couldn't do it and have one of them come and take over the lead.

I knew I had the rope and the gear to back me up if I fell, so the risk of injury was minimal. I had paid my dues rock climbing. I had the skills, and the move was within my ability. So what was the real issue? I was a very long way off the ground, that was really the only thing. But giving up was still very tempting, and I'd done it before. I could easily make up an excuse. I'd just say that I didn't feel up to it and I'd be off the hook, and it wouldn't matter, right? No, it would matter; I would know the truth. I would know that I—a big, tough

Himalayan climber—had chickened out on a stretch of rock that was well within my reach. I would have to live with knowing that I'd given in to my fear.

I took a deep breath, and moved back up onto the holds; I was at the decision point again. Go for it, or wimp out? A shout from below, "I've got you, go for it," was all I needed. Dave was assuring me that he had a good hold on the rope if indeed I fell, that there was really nothing to worry about. I decided that regardless of the void beneath my feet, this time it would be different. I made the decision to focus on solving the problem in front of me and forget everything else.

I had the hold in my left hand again, and it was unnerving not knowing what I'd find once I committed myself to the move. But I went for it and somehow found a decent hold with my right hand, brought my feet up to where my hand had been, and pulled over onto easier ground. "*Yee hah!*" I yelled. I had done it! I had broken through the barrier that I had backed away from so many times before. After a few more feet, I found a good place to anchor the rope and bring the guys up to join me. I had a moment alone to enjoy my victory. I was elated. The fear hadn't gone away; it was there all the time. I had simply decided to acknowledge it, accept it, put it in its place for a moment, and do what I needed to do. I was happy I had finished my lead, and proud I had done my part for the team, but I was on top of the world because I had broken through my fear and faced the challenge head on. The smile must have left a crease on my face.

High-altitude mountaineering is one of the world's most dangerous activities. Given that one in ten Himalayan climbers die on the mountains, it's understandable that climbers experience a great deal of fear. So who was I to think that I shouldn't have any fear, or that I couldn't be a great mountaineer because I struggled with it? One of the reasons I keep climbing is because I want to overcome and break through the fear that I experience. In many ways fear is still my worst enemy, but I know as I continue to put myself in those trying situations and face my fears head on, I'll continue to get the better of them.

People look at my climbing photos and say, "I could never do that; I'm afraid of heights." I'm sure most people have a fear of heights to some extent, and climbers are no different. Actors who have performed for years still get butterflies before a show, as do seasoned salespeople before a presentation. But they, like many climbers, have learned how to break through their fear, by doing what they have to do, over and over again. What's crucial is to be honest, stop making excuses for shortcomings and failures, and admit that you are afraid. It's OK! Many times I'd made phony excuses for my actions, and later felt disappointed with myself. I knew deep down that I had not only cheated and lied to myself, I'd often let other people down as well. My experience on El Cap taught me to be more aware of how I start to quit mentally before I reach my physical limits. I was letting fear get the best of me, which prevented me from finding out what I was actually capable of achieving. Soon,

I started to catch myself when I did the same thing in my day-to-day life, and I often see it when others gave in to their fear. You will not overcome your fear unless you are honest with yourself. Admit that the fear is there, and remember that experiencing fear is OK. This is the first step.

I have climbed with people who have mentally given up long before they reached their physical limits, in situations where they were quite safe and on climbs well within their abilities. It's disappointing to hear someone give every reason but the real one to explain why they didn't make it up a climb. No doubt some buy into their own excuses; many, unfortunately, never get out of that habit, and have a long list of climbs they "nearly" completed. These climbers diminish their self-images and belief in themselves as they deal with the frustration, shame, and guilt of not being truthful to themselves, not reaching the goals that they desire. I have faced fears in other areas of life, and I see people do the same thing in many of those arenas as well. Making a sales call, giving a presentation, changing career, risking romance after a failed marriage—all of these things require overcoming fear.

When you find yourself in an intimidating situation, it can be difficult to discern between fear and caution. It could be that your self-preservation instinct is warning you that real danger lurks nearby. If you heed these warnings and back down, you may later wonder which emotion it was, and whether you should have continued. Experience will teach you if the emotion you feel is instinct or fear, and then you can decide what to do in either situation.

While I am a great advocate of breaking through the fear barrier, I try to keep in mind that there are times when it is OK or even necessary to give in to fear. There are days when I go climbing and just don't feel quite right. I may feel disconnected, nervous, fearful—anything that makes me uneasy. I made the decision early in my climbing career to accept that I would have such days, and to be honest with my climbing partners and tell them what was going on. I learned that to try to ignore that feeling and continue might make me lose some of my nerve, and be worse off the next time I went climbing. Perhaps it's my body's way of telling me that today is not the day to "go for it," or perhaps it's my intuition telling me that something may be really wrong—such as bad weather or avalanche conditions. Whatever it is—fear, nerves, intuition, or the spicy Mexican food I had the night before—I always follow it; I'll even go home if necessary. At times like that, giving in to fear and not trying to overcome it is a smart thing to do. Knowing when you are having an off day, versus being in a frightening situation that you can and should push through, takes experience and truly tuning in to your feelings. Look at these days as learning experiences, not as failures.

I ask my climbing partners to be honest with me, and I want people I do business with and my friends to do the same.

If a climbing or business partner, or friend, tells me that they are fearful of something, I can deal with that and can often talk them through their fear, or I can take over and we can continue. I respect them for their honesty. But I don't like being given a phony excuse and having to retreat off a climb or project because they're not being honest with themselves or me. We can't deal with the real issue when it's hidden in a lie. There is no reason to go on, because there will be more excuses later, higher on the climb or deeper into the deal, when we are more committed and it's harder to retreat.

The result of that sort of deception (of yourself and others) is that you get in the habit of making excuses, and you stay controlled by fear. Once I understood this dynamic, I started noticing situations in my everyday life in which I'd experience the same fear I'd had on a climb, and my natural reaction would be to immediately back down. My strategy now is to quickly weigh the pros and cons of what I want to do, and accept the fact that there may be fear, doubt, and apprehension present. Then I remind myself that the consequences are probably not going to be as dramatic as they were on El Cap, so why not go for it?

Fear is an emotion you can control. When you look at fear as an essential element in an activity, you can allow it to keep you sharp, alert, and attentive. It heightens your senses, protects you, and can make you aware of things you may not otherwise have noticed. When you realize that you are experiencing a high level of fear and that it may be justified, you can accept that it doesn't make you less of a person, less of a climber, or less in any way. When you realize that it's acceptable and even understandable to have these feelings, then you can move on to the next step, which is to focus on the problem at hand. Do whatever scares you over and over again, and you will eventually gain a level of comfort and confidence with the activity. In this way, you control your fear.

Too many people give fear permission to paralyze them. They end up not asking for the date, not sticking their hand out to meet a new friend, not taking the trip, the job, the promotion. They let fear prevent them from leaving a bad relationship, a bad job, a city they hate, or an unsupportive friendship. Fear is a great stumbling block, preventing people from living the lives they deserve, from pursuing their dreams, because they are afraid they may fail. Many of our fears and worries are based on events that have not happened—and may never happen! The more you worry about what might happen, the more fear will freeze your action. You waste valuable energy visualizing an undesired outcome, which increases your sense of insecurity. Fear and doubt are often negative illusions, so replace them in your mind with the positive outcome that you desire. Victory over fear is achieved through action, and action will allow you to break through that barrier and achieve your goal.

Steps to overcoming your fear:

- When you experience fear, anxiety, worry, or apprehension, acknowledge your feelings.

- Accept that it is OK to experience any of these emotions, especially fear.

- Take responsibility—recognize and accept it when your fear causes you to back down and quit. Don't blame it on the weather, your gear, your partner, or anything else.

- Gauge whether your fear is justified or whether it is holding you back unnecessarily.

- Don't give the fear another thought—focus your attention on the task and your goal.

- Do the activity you fear as often as possible, for action cures fear.

The Sixth Lesson

EXPLORE YOUR LIMITS

Explore your limits with courage, faith, and humility.

—MARK ALLEN, *WORLD CHAMPION TRIATHLETE*

*F*inally, everything was as ready as it could be, and five of us set out from the 17,500-foot base camp to make our bid for the summit of the world's highest peak. We climbed through the icefall together without incident and moved past Camp One to Camp Two at 22,000 feet. Eager to move further up the mountain, we crawled into our sleeping bags right after dinner to try to get a decent night's sleep, but were woken by the sound of gale-force winds higher on the mountain. After peeking from the tent, Rick, our expedition leader, made the decision to wait another day for better conditions. I thought it would be smarter for us to move up to Camp Three, which was protected from the wind, but kept my opinion to myself and lay back down to wait for the sun to hit our tents. I wasn't sleeping well and the long night seemed to drag on forever. We spent the next day in our tents, reading, relaxing, eating, and hydrating, but I knew this inactivity would mean another restless night. I was ready to move!

We woke early again the next morning to the same high winds roaring over the South Col above us, and again Rick made the decision to wait another day. I wondered how much time we had left. I was starting to feel claustrophobic from being tentbound for so long. The next day was the same story. One more day *here and I knew I'd have to go down or I'd go crazy! I preferred to climb quickly, and these long nights followed by slow days with nothing to do were getting the best of me, even though I knew impatience could kill you quickly on Everest. Over dinner, Rick proposed that regardless of the winds we needed to move up. Instead of staying at Camp Three, the normal tactic for an ascent of Everest, he suggested we go all the way to Camp Four so that we could head for the summit if and when the winds died down. I didn't like the idea of going that far in one day, but once again kept quiet. The wind was less severe the next morning and we took off, heading up the relentless Lhotse face.*

⌐

Many a mountaineer's desire to explore his or her limits has led to feats that were previously considered impossible. In 1910, for example, two Alaskan miners climbed to the top of the 19,470-foot North Peak of Denali (the Native Alaskan name for Mount McKinley, which means "the High One"). They believed that America's highest peak should first be climbed by locals, rather than by "foreigners." From the swampland below, they wrongly thought this north peak to be the true summit. Though they had no mountaineering experience, their ascent concluded with an amazing 8,000-foot push from their highest camp to the top of the North Peak—in one day! The ascent was dismissed as a barroom fable until the fourteen-foot spruce pole they carried was spotted two years later by another team during the first ascent of Denali's true top, the 20,320-foot (South) summit.

I had heard stories about Denali, but I had climbed 20,000-foot peaks in Nepal in a single morning from their bases, so I couldn't fathom taking that long, or see what the big deal was about this mountain. By world standards, Denali is not especially high—measured above sea level, that is. However, no other mountain on earth towers as high over its base as Denali (plus, due to the reduced depth of the atmosphere at the poles, it feels more like 23,000 feet would feel in the Himalayas). I have a good friend who lost all his fingers and toes to frostbite on Denali, and another who took fifty-six days to climb it due to horrendously bad weather. Climbing Denali involves surviving huge crevasses, ferocious storms, and extremely cold conditions. In 1978 two Americans claimed a one-day ascent of Denali, but the claim didn't set a true record as they started halfway up the peak at 10,000 feet.

I wanted to really test myself, and wondered if it was humanly possible to cover the 13,000 feet and sixteen miles from the true base of the mountain (the 7,000-foot base camp and landing strip) to the 20,320-foot summit—in one day. It is a tremendous challenge to cover such an improbable distance on such a cold mountain. The idea soon became my obsession.

Out of the blue, I was invited to join Dr. Peter Hackett, the world-renowned high-altitude physiologist, to help out with his next research team on Mount McKinley. This was the opportunity I needed to get up there and attempt my one-day ascent. In collaboration with the Denali National Park Service, Dr. Hackett had manned a research and rescue post at 14,000 feet on Denali for the previous five years. A neverending stream of altitude-sick climbers were rescued and then tested at the post with drugs and procedures for high-altitude adaptation and acute mountain sickness.

I had three months to train and prepare for my world-record attempt—the first one-day ascent of North America's highest peak. I spent three weeks helping Dr. Hackett, after which time I was well acclimatized and ready to try a speed ascent. After one unsuccessful attempt with Trevor Pilling, an old climbing friend, I teamed up with Peter Athans, a friend from Colorado, who was eager to try something outrageous like a speed ascent. Pete, a fellow mountain guide in Nepal, has since climbed Everest seven times, more than any other Westerner.

As we made our attempt, we were stopped by strong winds at 16,000 feet and once again returned to my research tent at 14,000 feet. This camp was starting to feel like home. Pete and I were resting, having climbed through the night, when we were awakened by hysterical shouts from some climbers who had found two of their team dead in their tents, asphyxiated by fumes from their stove. We volunteered to help sled the two two hundred-pound corpses down to the landing strip, which took two very tiring days. A helicopter flew in to evacuate the bodies, and the pilot offered Pete and me a lift into town and back the next day, which we accepted.

At 2:00 P.M. the following afternoon, I left the airstrip at the small town of Talkeetna and flew back to the landing strip at base camp, but this time alone. I'd decided to try for a solo one-day ascent. Climbing alone would be far more dangerous, especially on the heavily crevassed glacier, but I would be able to focus all my energy on what I was doing, and wouldn't be distracted by ropes or a partner. I was fit, acclimatized, and as ready as I'd ever be. If it was indeed possible, and the altitude didn't get to me, the only other ingredient I needed was perfect weather, a rarity on Denali. I left the 7,000-foot Base Camp at 5:45 P.M. with a sleeping bag, down jacket, Gore-Tex jacket and pants, over-mitts, spare socks, a thermometer, two quarts of water, two bagels, and two candy bars. I had no stove or tent, no first aid kit or radio, nothing really to fall back on. I had to travel light, because there's no way one can do a rapid ascent carrying anything but the absolute essentials—it simply doesn't work.

The lower glacier went by easily, and I changed from my skis to crampons at the camp at 11,000 feet as everyone there slept. Luckily there was no wind at the infamous Windy Corner, as even without it the temperature dipped to −30°F.

My loneliest moment was at 3:00 A.M., when the midnight sun had gone down and it was dark, and I realized that if I slipped or fell in a crevasse there was no one around to help me. I watched every step. I moved through the camp at 14,000 feet and dropped my sleeping bag in my tent, then climbed quickly up the fixed ropes on the headwall above in an attempt to stay warm. The ridge between 16,000 and 17,000 feet went without a hitch; the sun had come up again and I had to grin at the perfect weather I could see in every direction. The climb to Denali Pass at 18,000 feet was in the shade and very cold, my thermometer read –40°F. Once again I was glad there was no wind. Once back in the sun I left my down jacket at the Pass, had a bagel and a drink, and headed for the summit.

My world became nothing but the sound of my breath. My mind became detached. I didn't feel the pain or exhaustion in my legs from the long rescue the days before, or the burning in my lungs from the cold, thin air. I climbed in a meditative trance, moving by instinct, effortlessly. My mind was completely relaxed, divorced from my body, focused only on each deep breath. It was as if I was floating above my physical body, which had become a huge moving lung. I saw myself drifting along, trying to sneak past the altitude so it wouldn't catch me. I moved so efficiently that my feet barely cleared the surface of the snow; the rest of my body was completely relaxed and not using an extra molecule of oxygen. I climbed automatically. I scanned the wind, the temperature, the snow, the route ahead—all were fine. I pushed hard, my heart rate high but controlled, my breathing deep and deliberate and in sync with every step.

One false summit after another on the summit ridge tortured me until there were no more. I snapped out of my trance as I realized that I had made it! I lifted my arms in a victory pose while I whooped and hollered, enjoying the moment and the incredible view. There wasn't a cloud for miles—it was a perfect day. It was 12:15 P.M., June 12, 1986, and I had achieved the first true one-day ascent of Mount McKinley in a world-record eighteen-and-a-half hours. I dug my ice axe into the snow, laid back on my pack, closed my eyes, and took a nap.

From years and years of climbing mountains, I knew my comfort level on high-altitude peaks. I knew where my climbing strengths lay, and where my weaknesses were. I decided to focus on my strengths and what I enjoy doing, regardless of what other climbers think or do, and to push myself by finding challenges within those parameters. The sense of freedom I felt from making that decision was huge!

Flying out from the landing strip on McKinley I looked back and could make out the route I had just taken. Earlier, heading straight down from the summit, I had seen the Cassin Ridge, an extremely steep and intimidating climb that is a formidable challenge, and a treasured prize for world-class mountaineers. I knew that I was technically skilled and experienced enough to climb that more difficult route, but I also knew that during my record ascent I had discovered my niche. I had found the type of climbing that I loved, that would challenge me to train hard, and in which I could excel. I knew I'd never be the best technical climber in the world, but I could make my mark in other ways that were more suited to my abilities. Tackling moderate routes on big peaks, in record time, by myself, would be how I would explore my limits.

While mastering skills, we often must do things that we don't like or don't do well, until we have at least some basic proficiency for our widening repertoires. It's while training and experimenting that we learn what we can and cannot do—and once we've identified our strengths, we can discover our true limits. Few people ever learn how much they are truly capable of, because they hold back and don't fully challenge themselves.

Remember that when personal risk is involved you must use common sense, and evaluate the risk in light of the reward. It's easy to get into trouble when your ambition exceeds your skill and experience. Exploring limits must be tempered by clearly knowing your true abilities. The time to test limits is when you have learned the lessons of the preceding chapters, and are searching for a way to stay motivated, to challenge yourself, and to move to a higher level of achievement.

You can have great adventure in your life by exploring your limits within any field or area of expertise. Whether you are a painter, a dancer, a climber, or a teacher—striving for excellence within your discipline will give your form of expression more power. Find what you love to do, what you do well, and then gather your courage and challenge yourself in that area. Don't try to please others or meet their expectations of you. Live your own life. The fun and excitement come from trying, from pushing yourself, from learning new things, and from attempting something that will give you confidence to try even greater things when the time is right. We all have limits, but few people learn what theirs are, because most give in too soon. Worthwhile achievement is hard; it takes effort, and that's what stops many people from trying.

Even if you are a high achiever and have accomplished incredible things in your life, you still need to find a way to keep motivated. To keep the adventure in your life, and to stay excited about what you are doing, you must continue to find activities that challenge you. Halfway up a rock face or a big mountain, or in the middle of writing a book or starting a business or a family, it's easy to get discouraged and give up— either mentally or physically, or both. You have to want to do it, even though it's hard.

When seeking motivation, look to those who are the best in the field for inspiration, but don't compare yourself negatively with people whose skill surpasses yours. View them as examples of where you can be if you continue to apply yourself. To learn more about what steps to tackle next, look more to people with your level of skill and expertise. By watching the way others develop their skills, you can develop a plan—with a timeline—to reach higher levels of performance. Learning to set a realistic pace to reach goals is extremely important, as I explain in the eighth lesson.

Exploring your limits means finding that place where you are stretching yourself beyond what you believe—or may have once believed—is possible. Keeping a high level of motivation comes from maintaining a level of performance and adventure in your life that keeps you excited enough to keep going. If your goal doesn't challenge you, you will get bored and quit. (But don't let yourself get discouraged by choosing an objective that is too far out of reach, and causes you to give up early or not put all your effort into your activity.) Choose an objective for which the outcome is uncertain, so that you maintain a sense of adventure that keeps you motivated. It's the "not knowing" that keeps you going, and makes life an adventure.

Steps to exploring your limits:

- Determine where you feel comfortable, where your strengths lie in your chosen field.
- Consider in what areas you could push yourself for a real challenge.
- Establish a level of performance that exceeds your comfort level and excites you.

- As much as possible, stop the activities you don't like or that you are doing because of others' expectations. (You still might have to take out the trash!)
- Recognize when you are at your peak readiness, and maximize the moment.

The Seventh Lesson

CHOOSE YOUR PARTNERS WISELY

When you're down and out,

surround yourself with people you like.

—**David Breashears,** *mountaineer, adventurer,*
and **IMAX** *filmmaker*

*T*he Lhotse Face is a steep, mile-high wall that requires difficult and sustained ice climbing to ascend to Camp Three, which is located on a precariously carved, ice-encrusted perch at 24,000 feet. Tents are dug into the only available place on the face: a number of narrow ledges that are protected from frequent avalanches by the fifty-foot high ice cliffs. Expeditions push to get to this area early in the season to get a decent spot in this tiny oasis of safe ground. We had spread ourselves out on the face, climbing separately up the fixed ropes from Camp Two to Camp Three, which is often the way teams climb on Everest. Once a team has fixed their ropes, climbers clip onto the fixed ropes and move at their own pace.

Three of our team arrived at Camp Three ahead of me, had already melted snow and filled their water bottles, and were leaving the camp as I arrived. I wished the guys good luck and told them I'd see them at Camp Four. We had a long way to go, and I didn't feel well at all. I was moving more slowly than normal and I wanted to get going as soon as possible, but it took forever at this altitude to melt enough snow to fill my water bottle. Rick, bringing up the rear, arrived at the tent just as I was about to leave. Without thinking, I handed him the water bottle I had just filled. He nodded, thanked me, and headed off. I went

back to the tent, and as I relit the stove the conse-
quences of what I had just done hit me.

~

Though the lessons in this book hold true in any environment, amidst the inherent danger of the mountains they stand out more than they do in everyday life. When your life is at stake, choosing your partners wisely is one of the most important preparations you can make, as the following story illustrates.

I first met Trevor Pilling on the trail in Nepal and we quickly hit it off. Trevor was a member of the elite British SAS, the Special Air Service, and he was frequently on assignment in exotic locations. When he wasn't on a dangerous mission he was "training," as he called it, on a mountain somewhere. I ran into him all over the world: on Mount McKinley in Alaska, numerous times in Nepal, and rock climbing in Yosemite Valley in California. The SAS are very tough, but Trevor also had a soft side.

I'll never forget the last time I saw Trevor. One of my trekking groups was having the obligatory post-trek celebratory dinner in the notorious Rum Doodle Bar in Kathmandu, when he walked in. He had just completed his expedition and walked straight to the Rum Doodle for a drink. Trevor had a powerful presence; always the gentleman, he introduced himself to everyone at the table, making jokes as he went.

"How did it go?" I asked excitedly, referring to his last expedition, expecting news of their success.

He paused, let out a long sigh, and I watched the color drain from his face. In his best British stiff-upper-lip manner, he calmly replied, "It was a tragedy."

After an uncomfortable moment of silence, I asked, "Gosh mate, what happened?"

"Phil didn't make it," came his terse answer.

Phil was Trevor's climbing partner and best friend. They had met as schoolboys, when Trevor had rescued him in a snowstorm in the Scottish Highlands. They had spent their early years rock climbing all over England and, like me, had inevitably made their way to the Himalayas.

We all offered our sympathy, and gave Trevor a safe place to unload the story of the nightmare he had been through. He started at the end.

"It took me two very long and dangerous days to climb back down the glacier to safety. I should have been elated, but I tried to hide my tears as the two other members of our climbing team reached me. No words were exchanged as they grabbed my pack. I started sobbing again when they turned and headed back to Base Camp and I realized they weren't going to go back up for Phil." We hung on every word.

"Phil and I accepted a far too tempting last-minute invitation from two Welsh climbers, Mark and Steve, who had permission to climb a new route on Annapurna South [a

24,000-foot peak in central Nepal]. It wasn't until we reached our Base Camp that it became clear they weren't sufficiently experienced and needed us to give them any chance of success. But it was too late to do anything about it. We climbed and worked in teams of two, alternating between pushing our route further up the mountain, and resting and sorting gear at Base Camp. Mark and Steve came back down to rest after establishing a third camp at 20,000 feet. Phil and I took off the next day, hoping to establish a fourth camp at 22,500 feet, so that all four of us would be in striking distance of the summit.

"Phil and I climbed up to and stayed overnight at the third camp, and left at dawn the next morning to open up new terrain for our team. The sky was dark with clouds and by noon a blizzard was upon us. We'd just climbed a very steep wall of ice and there was nowhere to put our tent. In desperation we crawled into a crevasse in the ice, which wasn't deep enough to protect us from the blowing snow, but which kept us out of the full force of the wind. It was too cramped to light our stove so we just ate some dried fruit and tried to sleep. In the morning Phil seemed distant, and we didn't talk much. I thought he was just cold and hungry after a bad night. I asked him to hold the rope for me as I climbed back out onto the face to find a place to cook something and get some sleep.

"All I could find was a sloping ledge on which I dug a small snow cave. I thought Phil would let me know if he wanted to help, so when he was silent I assumed he wanted to rest. Digging took me most of the morning and when I climbed back to Phil I was shocked at what I saw. He was lying outside his sleeping bag in a pool of vomit. He mumbled incoherently and stared at me blankly. I didn't know what else to do, but pack our gear as quickly as I could. It wasn't difficult to get back to the cave but Phil was so slow it was dark by the time we arrived. As I helped him get settled I realized he'd urinated in his pants. This was getting serious. I tried to call the guys at Base Camp on the radio but the batteries were too cold to work.

"I still don't know what was wrong with him. Phil was speaking gibberish as I changed him into dryer clothes and put him into his sleeping bag. I pleaded with him to eat and drink, knowing he was rapidly losing strength. It was like trying to feed a baby who wouldn't cooperate. If he didn't drink he'd become even more dehydrated, making the effects of high altitude and hypothermia worse. We were trapped by the storm for the next two days and I spent every moment melting snow, trying to force-feed Phil and keep him warm and dry. He went in and out of consciousness, only occasionally making sense. We were almost out of food and fuel, and it was obvious we had to get out of there, quickly. Having warmed up the batteries in my jacket, I radioed Mark and Steve at base camp and, trying to hide the concern in my voice from Phil, told them we *really* needed help. They assured me they'd be up once the storm cleared. I worried that might be too late.

"On the third morning the wind and snow had stopped—time to go! Staying meant certain death for both of us. I tried to get Phil moving but quickly realized that since he couldn't stand up he wouldn't be able to climb down a 4,000-foot ice face. By now I was getting weak, and since we only had one rope our only hope was help from below. I radioed down to ask Dawa, our Sherpa cook, when Mark and Steve had gone, but Steve answered. I yelled into the radio demanding to know why they hadn't left yet. In a very slow and rehearsed tone, Steve told me they weren't coming, that it was too dangerous. What bunk! I tried to explain that the ridge we were on was too steep to be avalanche prone, but they didn't want to listen. I pleaded with them that they *had* to risk it. We would die if they didn't come and help me get Phil down!

"I couldn't believe that they were unwilling to at least try to help us. I helped Phil put his harness and crampons on, got my own gear ready, and took a look out of the cave at the sickening void below us. This was crazy. Phil couldn't even stand up. I racked my brain for a solution, weighing the options in my mind. Phil couldn't rappel down the rope, and trying to lower him would be futile. I could stay here with him and we would both die, as it would take the others a couple of days to reach us. Or, I could go down and leave Phil here, an option I didn't even want to think about. I really wanted to get out of there, especially since the weather was better and I didn't know how long that would last, but I decided to wait one more day for the others to come up. I was already very dehydrated and had a bad headache from the altitude. I knew that another day could mean I might not have the strength to get out of there myself, but I couldn't bring myself to leave.

"First thing the next morning I looked down the face, but there was no sign of the others. I didn't even bother calling them on the radio. I looked over at Phil, but his eyes gave back nothing. I knew what I had to do. I had to go down alone and try to convince them to come back up for Phil. I knew he wouldn't last long on his own, not at this altitude. I made Phil as comfortable as possible, and put the stove and the little food that was left beside him. He looked right at me and I sensed a peace, an understanding between us, and I knew that it was OK. He wanted me to go down just as I would want him to go down if the situation were reversed. I tried not to think anymore, but the question kept pestering me, I didn't have a choice, did I? DID I? I fought back my tears, gave him a squeeze on the shoulder, and said, 'Hang in there, mate.' I turned and left, without my best friend. It was the hardest thing I've ever had to do."

People casually toss around the word "friend," but I believe that friendship, true friendship, must be developed and earned. It's not automatic just because two people hit it off. A friend is someone who won't let you down, no matter what. I've learned not to risk my life with people unless I really know them. I don't expect others to take risks for me unless I have some history with them. Mark and Steve were part of a climbing team with no history or relationship bonding them all together. They decided not to risk their lives for people with whom they had no long-term relationship or connection. Trevor and Phil made a very costly mistake by choosing to go on an extremely dangerous undertaking without really knowing their teammates.

In climbing, being compatible means that you climb at approximately the same level as your partner—but more importantly, it means that you have different strengths from which you can both benefit. This holds true in many other areas of life. I have learned through many tough lessons to wisely choose the people with whom I spend time, whether it's climbing, doing business, or socializing. Whenever possible, I surround myself with people whose company I enjoy, and who have a positive outlook. Life is too short to spend with anyone who offers you less. I choose to hang out with people who believe in me and in my goals, dreams, and aspirations, and I avoid negative people, who have a pessimistic outlook on life or on what I'm trying to accomplish. My good friends know that they can share their candid opinions with me when I get too far off base, and I welcome that. I strongly believe in having many mentors in my life, people I can go to with ideas and get *honest* opinions from. I also am brutally honest with my friends, and they know that I will tell them the truth and not shrink from what I believe is right. Others will rarely be as honest with them, because of fear of rejection or of provoking anger.

What you are looking for in a climbing partner, or a business or life partner, is someone you can trust, respect, rely on, and enjoy being with, and someone with whom you can be yourself. I've spent some of the most miserable times in my life on climbing trips with people with whom I realized I had nothing in common except the climb. The most important aspect of life is your relationships, so why compromise your standards with your life partner, your friends, or the people with whom you work and do business? The people you surround yourself with should contribute to your achievements. You can choose to share your dreams with people who will be honest with you and want you to succeed. Go for the best, take no chances—choose wisely, and selectively. Remember, it is your life!

Few of us in everyday life are faced with the sort of tough, life-and-death decisions that Trevor and his teammates had to make. Yet we all must choose with whom we ascend life's great mountains, including our workmates, spouses, and friends. We should make each of these choices carefully and thoughtfully, and put together our winning "team." I urge you to take your time and choose wisely. A poor choice can be deadly!

NOTE: Trevor Pilling and his life partner Sara went missing in Nepal in 1992 while allegedly attempting to climb, Mount Machapuchare, a sacred mountain. It is not known whether they were swept away by an avalanche, or murdered by thieves—

or by locals who were protecting their sacred mountain. Their bodies were never found. Trevor was one of the few people in the world I could really call a friend. I knew he was someone who would do anything for me, even if it meant risking his own life to save mine (as he did once on Mount McKinley in Alaska). I miss them both.

Steps to choosing your partners wisely:

- Accept that true friendship is rare, and must be developed over time.

- Be cautious and selective about who you spend time and take risks with.

- Try to surround yourself with people who uplift you and believe in you.

- Seek mentors who will encourage, yet be brutally honest with you. This is the kind of person who will help you achieve your dreams.

- Choose wisely with whom you share your life, your business, and your dreams.

| The Eighth Lesson |

FIND YOUR PACE

... when a defining moment comes along,

you define the moment ...

or the moment defines you.

—ROY MCAVOY, *IN TIN CUP*

*A*t 24,000 feet it took me almost an hour to melt enough snow to fill another water bottle. But I surprised myself by catching up to Rick at the base of the 800-foot cliff known as the Yellow Band (named for the color of the rock). Rick was talking with one of our high-altitude climbing Sherpas who said he was sick and couldn't continue. The Sherpa was worried about his load, which the team needed. Rick and I looked at each other knowing we had a decision to make. The obvious thing to do was to split the load. But Rick was our expedition leader, and he had enough on his plate, so I made the quick decision to do whatever I could to help him and the team. I suggested that he get going and I would take the load. The Sherpa descended and Rick headed up. By the time I found room in my pack for the twenty-pound load (which felt like an extra sixty pounds at that altitude), I realized that I had given up my shot for the summit—I would be too exhausted to continue when I reached the final camp.

With help from bottled oxygen, Rick moved much faster than I could with my extra load, and he gradually climbed out of sight. Now I was really alone. I noticed that the sky was now covered in dark clouds, and I knew I had to get going. But I couldn't; my chest infection was slowing me to a pace of one step, ten

breaths, another step, and another ten breaths. I won-
dered if I would even be able to make it up the steep
rock band ahead of me. It took forever, but I made it,
and headed up the snowfield toward my final obsta-
cle, a 1,000-foot cliff called the Geneva Spur. By the
time I crossed the few hundred yards over to the base
of the spur it had started snowing heavily and a bone-
chilling wind had picked up. I thought about the
weather, the distance to the next camp, the effort
required to ascend the rock spur, how terrible I felt,
and how slowly I was moving. I wondered if it would
be smarter to turn around and go down instead of
going up any further.

⟿

By 1988 I had been going on a major expedition every two
years or so, working my way up toward my ultimate goal of
climbing Mount Everest. After Mount McKinley, I wanted
to raise the bar and set a greater challenge for myself.
I decided to go for one-day ascent records for the highest
mountain on each of the seven continents. Aconcagua was
next on the list. Mount Aconcagua, the "Jewel of the Andes,"
at 22,841 feet, is the highest peak outside Asia. On the border
of Chile and Argentina, and only three hours from a major
city, it's one of the easiest, most accessible, most popular, and

relatively "safest" high-altitude peaks in the world. Although more than a hundred people have died while climbing Aconcagua, the standard route is quite straightforward for experienced mountaineers. It has few objective hazards beyond sudden gale force winds and fierce snowstorms that can blow in unannounced from the Pacific Ocean (only a hundred miles away).

I had just finished guiding six other team members to the summit of Aconcagua. The ascent took us twelve days, which is enough time to acclimatize and ascend safely, while giving everyone on the team a chance to make it to the top. Some groups climb it a few days faster, but usually fewer members of those teams get to the top, due to altitude sickness, and those who do usually feel lousy on summit day. Now that I was acclimated, my goal was another world-record ascent, and I hoped to reach the summit in less than ten hours. As I had arranged with my coleader, once we had the team safely back at our base camp I would be free to try a speed ascent. I would then catch up with the team at the trailhead before they left for the airport. The rest of the team was still sleeping as I quietly dressed in the pre-dawn light. My pack, which weighed no more than ten pounds, was ready, so all I had to do was have something to eat and drink, fill my water bottles, and leave. Some of our group were awakened by the hissing noise of the stove. We shared a hot drink and some high-fives, as they wished me a safe and successful climb and I headed out of camp. As soon as

I reached the trail, heading steeply up and out of our Base Camp, I directed my focus to the task at hand.

I quickly passed the higher campsites our group had used. I took a few quick food and water breaks, and was moving at a fairly decent pace until I reached the bottom of the final section to the summit, at 21,000 feet. I knew I had chosen a pace that was well within my comfort zone, not pushing it too hard too early, but something was definitely wrong. I stopped at the high camp to change clothing and had to sit down to rest. I didn't know why but I felt wiped out, totally exhausted. Was it from the long descent the day before? I doubted it. The two days before my one-day ascent of McKinley I had spent dragging a two hundred pound body. And numerous times in the Himalayas I had broken unofficial ascent records, such as climbing 18,450-foot Kala Pattar (near Mt. Everest Base Camp) from its base in under thirty-five minutes, without having rested in the days beforehand. So what was the matter? Was I just having an off day?

On McKinley I had been completely relaxed, I realized. I had climbed in a trance-like state, finding a pace that worked for me and sticking with it, climbing as if on autopilot, and having a great time. On McKinley my mind had been blank and devoid of stress or pressure; I had simply done my thing. Here, on Aconcagua, I felt a tremendous amount of pressure to perform, to set another record. I realized that I was stressed-out over my goal, and that all that pressure and all

those expectations were burning energy and oxygen mole-
cules by the truckload. I couldn't stop my mind from chant-
ing, over and over again, "I've got to do this in eight hours."
Just the stress of worrying was wasting valuable oxygen. I had
essentially burned up energy reserves by trying too hard. This
caused tension in my muscles and wore me out more quickly
than normal.

I could have kept going, as many summit-possessed
mountaineers do, but I knew I probably wouldn't have the
energy to get back down if I did. The weather was stable, but I
was a mess. Physically I still had some energy left, but mentally
I was totally spent. Disappointed, I turned around and went
down, even though I was less than 1,000 feet below the summit. My record attempt would have to wait until another day.
I arrived back at Base Camp at nightfall and collapsed into my
tent, too tired to eat. I left the next morning with the rest of the
team but hiked by myself, contemplating what I had learned
from this experience. I don't remember much of the bus ride
to the airport, or the long flight home.

There was a period in my early twenties when I lived in
South Australia and rock-climbed full time, six days a week. It
was an amazing time in Australian climbing history, as many of
the best climbers from around the country were living there
and pushing the limits on the local cliffs. When we weren't
climbing we were training, and the competitive atmosphere
was intense. I wanted to be the best climber in Australia more

than anything, but I could never climb better than fellow climber Kim Carrigan. I thought about being the best *all* the time, and one day it dawned on me that perhaps I was trying too hard. I was wasting energy thinking about being the best, while Kim's energy was focused on his climbing. He didn't worry about being better than anyone else, he just relaxed and did his thing, and climbed because he loved it. Kim went on to become one of the best rock climbers in the world.

When you try too hard it often just gets in the way. You can also not try hard enough, of course. The key is to know through training and experience what the right pace is, for you and for your goal. Sure, it's fine to dream about being the best, a world champion, an Olympic Gold medalist, a record holder—but an obsession with winning may limit you, rather than help you. At the Olympics, many athletes put too much pressure on themselves, and the media compound the problem by adding their own expectations. This increased stress can hamper an athlete's performance. Those who relax and just do their best because they love the sport, often do better than more gifted athletes who think they have something to prove.

In mountaineering, trying too hard is a fatal mistake, especially at high altitudes, because it uses up precious oxygen essential for survival. When I lead trips I suggest that my clients relax and enjoy the trip, and leave the worrying to me. Our schedule is carefully designed to allow the group to fully acclimatize, and I therefore recommend that they not worry about the altitude. Worrying about it accomplishes nothing. In fact it only adds to the problem. Once you decide what you need to do, the secret is to just relax and do it.

Years ago, when I was in radio advertising sales, I found that when I was too attached to the outcome of the sale I never did very well. When I tried too hard I would sometimes manipulate the sale to my advantage, and it rarely worked out for the client or for me. It's almost like the customer could smell my desperation for the sale and would run the other way. It's when I relaxed and almost didn't care what happened that I did the best. By being detached from the outcome sales happened naturally—and they were always the easiest sales and became the relationships that lasted the longest.

I've also seen this same principle in practice when people are on the hunt for a relationship. If they enter into "negotiations" too attached to the final goal, it prevents interactions from naturally unfolding. The result is stifling (even to a couple who might have made a good match), or it may lead to serious involvement before a couple knows whether they are really good for each other.

Some cars have a fuel economy gauge that lets the driver see the optimal speed of travel. Sometimes speeding up or slowing down is necessary to reach optimum fuel economy. Our bodies work in the same way, and at high altitudes or under extreme conditions, exaggerated and minute adjustments are critical. Finding your optimum pace allows you to use less energy, burn less oxygen, and climb longer and faster. It's amazing how well the body and mind work when they're operating at the optimum pace. Find the tempo that allows you to operate almost effortlessly and stay there. At this point you will use less energy than if you increase or decrease your pace. A mountaineer's pace is slow and steady with very few rests, and he or she can go all day—just like the tortoise that beat the hare!

You can find your pace by experimenting; it is determined by your ultimate goal. Athletes who have the luxury of a coach often train using heart-rate monitors, to establish a specific training and competing speed and intensity. I am not that sophisticated. I go by feel, and use my experience. I have run up trekking peaks in Nepal countless times, and from that I have learned how my body responds at different speeds. Training allows you to know what your body can and cannot do, so that you have a much more accurate idea of your optimum pace when in competition.

When going for any goal, choose a timeframe that challenges you to perform at your best, that keeps you on the edge (and therefore excited and motivated)—but that is not so ambitious that you get discouraged and give up. Once you've established your objective, you can relax and go at a speed that will work for you. Rushing things often leads to disaster. The success rate on Aconcagua, and on most technical mountains for that matter, is less than fifty percent, and the reason that most people do not reach the summit is inadequate acclimatization: they go too high too fast. Success in any endeavor is difficult enough without adding more stress. Just give it your best shot. Though there are times when your body wants to quit and your mind must take over, you just have to pick a pace and relax into it.

Competitive people may find it difficult to resist trying to keep up with someone else, even when they know the pace is beyond their abilities. The benefits of exploring your limits are entirely lost if you focus on trying to look good to someone else. Similarly, pressure and unreasonably high expectations often override talent and skill, leading to failure. Rushing frequently causes mistakes. There is a big difference between moving quickly and efficiently, and rushing around as fast as possible. In business and personal relationships, rushing is often perceived by others as pressure, and they may respond with resistance that wouldn't be there otherwise.

Although taking risks is often part of working toward big goals, you must take those risks when you know that the time is right. There are athletes who have gone all out and taken the risk of pushing themselves beyond what they should, and many mountaineers have gambled with their lives as well. Sometimes the risk pays off with the success of a gold medal or a summit, but often the risk means paying the ultimate price.

Weigh the risks and then decide. Few voluntary activities have such monumental consequences as a mistake on the high mountains of the world. A few athletes each year pull off amazing feats through skill, bravado, and a good measure of luck, but for the rest of us who don't want to risk everything, it's better to pick a pace that will allow us to achieve our objectives safely. You don't want to lose your shirt from one bad investment, or ruin a relationship with a client or coworker because of a reckless decision.

If you find yourself worrying about not achieving your goal, it's important to find ways to quiet those doubts and regain your equilibrium. Meditation, yoga, visualization, a personal mantra—use anything that allows you to remember your long-term goals and to tap into your feelings of self-confidence. Systems for calming and regaining control over your mind can be cultivated over time, as I discuss in the tenth lesson.

When you find your optimal pace, you can relax and begin transferring energy to your task. Try to maintain your own pace, one that you can maintain throughout the entire project, leaving enough in reserve to finish. It's important not to exhaust yourself mentally or physically at any time. Part of being true to yourself is to set your goals and achieve them at your own pace, using your own schedule, and not to allow anyone else to set the pace for you. Training and experience will help you accomplish this.

Steps to finding your pace:

- Determine a realistic plan, and a timeframe in which to achieve your goals, both short- and long-term.
- Figure out the right pace you will need to maintain to accomplish your objective.
- Believe that you *will* accomplish your goal if you simply follow your plan and strike the right pace.
- Know yourself. Do your thing. Relax and don't worry, and enjoy the journey.

| The Ninth Lesson |

FOLLOW YOUR INSTINCTS

I believe in an extra-consciousness that looks after you.

It only comes into play in extreme circumstances,

which for me is in the mountains.

—ROGER MARSHALL, *A FRIEND WHO DIED ON EVEREST IN 1987*

I *looked down and saw that the Yellow Band was completely covered in a slippery layer of snow. Descending would be difficult and dangerous, plus I was carrying a load of food that the team needed, and this gave me the impetus to keep moving. Getting the food to the team to help them get to the top became my new vision. Leading upwards, the fixed rope was anchored every hundred feet or so. All I could do in my weakened condition was to focus on getting to the next anchor point.*

The steep face took everything I had. My crampons scraped against the bare, glacier-worn rock, searching for a foothold. I moved excruciatingly slowly, each breath a struggle in the thin air, made more painful by my debilitating chest problems. The temperature had dropped significantly, and if I stopped moving for a second I could feel the cold attacking every part of my body. I had my head down and didn't notice how hard it was snowing or how much the wind had picked up. By the time I reached the top of the spur and stuck my head over the ridge it was dark. I was met with gale force winds against which I had to steady myself to keep my balance. The fixed rope ended, so I unclipped from it, now even more at risk of being blown off the ridge. I had expected to clip immediately back onto another fixed rope, but there was none to be found. The blizzard stopped me from seeing more than a few feet in front of me. Going a few steps in every direction, I was trying not to lose my footing on the steep terrain. I searched desperately for the next fixed rope, my safety line, and my way to the next camp, until I realized that I'd missed it. All I could do was head off into the storm in what I thought—and hoped—was the right direction.

⌒

Instinct is not something that you can be taught. This inner intuitive voice, your internal radar or sixth sense, is a powerful tool that some people learn to develop naturally. Those who cultivate it, put in the time, master the skills, and gain the experience, can listen to this inner voice for guidance. Because I've been attentive to my instincts and chosen to follow them over my doubts and fears, my instincts have gotten stronger over time, and have helped me out of countless scrapes. One dramatic example of this happened one lovely spring in the Annapurna Range of the Himalayas, when I led a group of ten—myself, six climbers, a cook, and two climbing Sherpas—in a potentially deadly expedition. I'm grateful that by that time my instincts were well honed; if they hadn't been, none of us would have survived.

The first day started out bright and sunny, and we laughed and enjoyed each other's company as we hiked up the final grassy hillside to a snowfield where we placed our high camp. The porters who had accompanied us dropped their loads of tents, food, fuel, and climbing equipment at our perch, high above the Annapurna Sanctuary—a cirque-shaped valley enclosed on all sides by spectacular mountains—and headed back down. The team busied itself preparing for the next day, as the Sherpas set up the tents and our cook started dinner. Our goal was Tent Peak—at 18,045 feet, the lowest of the eighteen nonexpedition peaks that you can get permission to climb in Nepal, but far from the easiest.

During dinner I noticed a dark, sinister-looking cloud moving over us from the north—the only direction in which we hadn't been able to see very far from base camp. I didn't like the look of that cloud one bit.

It was snowing by the time we went to bed. I had never seen such large, wet snowflakes, let alone snow that fell that heavily. I couldn't sleep, and looked outside every few hours to check the conditions. By midnight we'd had three feet of snow. I got dressed and woke the Sherpas and the rest of the group. We took turns clearing snow away from the tents and I tried to allay everyone's concerns. Amazingly, by 4:00 A.M., the time we had planned to start climbing, the gathering snow was now level with the tops of our tents. We couldn't dig it away fast enough. I discussed our options with the Sherpas, none of which were very good. We had brought extra food, but realistically only had enough for two more days at best.

I waded back to the tents and told the group that I didn't like the idea of being pinned down here by the storm for an indefinite time. The thought of sitting in our tents waiting to get buried by an avalanche wasn't very appealing. I expected that the storm would last a while, and that we should go down before things got any worse, but there were ten lives on the line, and I wanted everyone to be able to voice their opinion. Everyone wanted to go down, though they knew the danger was severe either way. I made the decision to descend.

To get everyone down safely we would need to travel lightly and move quickly, so I made the call to leave the tents and most of the climbing equipment and ropes behind. With the extreme avalanche danger, roping the team together would be too dangerous. This would be an expensive trip for me, but getting us all out alive was far more important than saving the gear. By 6:00 A.M., when we were ready to go, the snow was so deep I had to cut a hole in the top of my tent to get out. Fortunately, most of the team was in good spirits, and they joked and sang songs with the Sherpas to help break the tension.

It took a huge effort to push a trail through the waist-deep snow. The whiteout conditions and cloud cover prevented us from seeing more than a few feet, and the constant roar of avalanches made us all very nervous. The snow slid continually from under our feet. Numerous times members of our group were swept down the slope and nearly over a 2,000-foot drop. Fortunately, I'd taught everyone how to stop themselves with their ice axes. This steep hillside was a deathtrap. We took turns crossing gullies and skirting avalanches that came every few minutes. I would yell "GO," and one of our team would race across to the other side of the gully. I really thought that someone was going to die, and I know they all thought that they could be the one. The tension was sky high, and one of the team members broke down and sobbed. It seemed that there were too many close calls for one not to be fatal. It would be a miracle if all of us got out of this alive.

Blinded by the blowing snow, the Sherpas argued about the safest way to go. I took over and tried my best to lead us down, but I couldn't see where I was going either. After about an hour in the lead I stopped suddenly in the thigh-deep powder and stood there—I don't know why. I held up my hand and everyone stopped and stood silently with me. I stood there for about ten minutes, and then suddenly the clouds and snow cleared. We were within two steps of a cliff with a 1,500-foot drop.

Late in the afternoon we finally reached the bottom of the snow-covered hillside, but we still had to cross the rock-covered glacier to get to our base camp. Low clouds prevented us from seeing any recognizable features, and the snow covered any trail that might have been there. We were all disoriented and the Sherpas continued to discuss which way we should go.

I took off and the team followed, too tired to argue. We were soon in a deep trough in the glacier but we may as well have been deep in the Sahara desert. In every direction there were undulating mounds of rock covered with a layer of snow, which looked like sand dunes. Everything appeared the same, no matter which way you looked. There was nothing to help us get our bearings. I pushed on in what I believed was the right direction, guided only by instinct.

Finally someone asked me if I really knew where base camp was. I said, "Yes," and kept going. Soon there was another question, "Are you sure we're going the right way?" Once again I said, "Yes." Within another half-hour, the questions became so frequent that I stopped, turned around, and addressed the team. "You guys are throwing off my radar. Every time you ask me a question it throws me off and I start to doubt myself. I want to get out of here as much as you do and don't particularly want to spend any extra time wandering around on this glacier. Trust me, please; I'll get us back to camp." No one spoke another word, and within an hour or so we were all safely back at camp.

It is incredibly stressful to spend twelve straight hours being cold and wet and thinking you are going to die at any moment. We were so looking forward to warm clothing, sleeping in a dry tent, and a hot meal. But when we arrived at base camp, we were shocked to find that it had been ravaged by the storm. The tents had all but collapsed, and the Sherpas who had stayed behind had given the dry clothes in our duffel bags to the porters so that they could stay warm. (We couldn't fault them for that.) Everyone pitched in to salvage what we could of our camp, with most of our individual tents destroyed. By the time our cook had a much-anticipated hot meal of rice and lentils ready, we had repaired the large dining tent, which would be our home for the night. We all ate together: the team, the Sherpas, and the porters who hadn't fled once it started snowing, and we had a great evening sharing the adventure we had survived.

It took us three more days of trekking through deep snow and avalanche-prone territory before we could find a safe place to dry out. Everyone was thankful that we had left the high camp when we did, as the storm lasted for three more days. Back in Kathmandu, we learned that twenty-two climbers had died in that one storm.

Descending Tent Peak, I followed my instincts as well as I could. Despite all the anxiety and the obstacles, experience had taught me that I had what I needed to get through the ordeal, if I just listened deep inside myself. The more experience you have under your belt, the more you can tune in to your intuition. Many people make the mistake of allowing fear and doubt to cloud their true instincts. Experience and faith in yourself will teach you how to pay attention. Once you have learned to trust your radar, you can be certain that you will be all right in even the most trying circumstances. Sometimes that quiet but persistent inner voice will tell you, "This is the way. Follow me." Other times it will tell you, "Be careful, danger ahead." Your inner radar is the way the universe or your God can guide you. When you have a sense, a hunch, a feeling about something, follow it.

I distinctly remember how I felt when I first arrived at the Everest base camp in 1991. I looked up at Everest with two voices vying for priority in my head. In my left ear, a voice whispered, "Gary, you're not good enough. You are not ready for this. Maybe you should go home." In my right ear, another voice said; "Gary, you are in the best shape of your life. You have been on dozens of mountains in the Himalayas. Go for it—it's your time!"

I decided to stop listening to the voice in my left ear.

The voice you listen to the most is the one that grows stronger and becomes dominant. I used to think that having even a tiny bit of doubt meant something was wrong. Now I realize that doubt is normal, but that I can choose which voice to listen to. If I listen to the positive voice that plays most of the time, giving me confidence and belief in myself, I know that everything will be OK. Knowing that doubt and fear are normal makes it easier to move forward with confidence. Distinguishing the difference between your instincts and these other voices, and knowing which one to follow, comes down to experience.

In Western culture, we learn early to shut off our instinctual response, and instead develop our other five senses as a means of increasing our intellectual, emotional, and social skills. If we accept the reality of our intuitive side, we can consciously develop it. Observe and learn from your feelings, and learn to believe in yourself. It takes time to develop that sixth sense; it requires you to be open to hearing your inner voice, and willing to follow it. And it's well worth the time.

Animals are born with strong instincts to eat and reproduce, but they *become* intuitive enough to survive in the wilderness through experience and what they learn from their parents and other animals. Human intuitive abilities are developed in much the same way, by studying and learning, and by performing an activity over and over.

Before a trip, I warn my group members that we will probably meet dozens of other people on the trail, who will have had a wide range of experience. I suggest that while with me they listen to me, and that in the future, when on their own, they follow their own instincts—rather than blindly listening to the advice of someone whose level of experience or knowledge is unknown. When I first started climbing in the Himalayas, too often I ended up in trouble, and made stupid mistakes, because of listening to other people when I didn't know their experience level; I should have relied on my own experiences and followed my intuition, but I was young and inexperienced myself, and I thought that everyone knew better than I.

Early in my mountaineering career, I noticed that when I went on a trip by myself, I would feel apprehensive at the beginning. At first I wondered if my instincts weren't telling me to go back home. After a few solo trips, however, I realized that I was just feeling lonely and frightened about being alone. I had to learn over time to examine my feelings and decide what was going on. If the feeling of uneasiness kept up, then I would heed it, but if that feeling quickly subsided I would dismiss the uneasiness and move on to have a great climb. Nothing replaces experience in teaching you how to tell the difference between superficial feelings and your deeper intuition. Believe and trust in yourself.

Steps to following your instincts:

- Believe and trust in your instincts.
- Always make the best decision possible with the information you have available, based on your experiences, your reasoning, and your intuition.
- Develop your instincts. Practice makes you better.
- Learn to distinguish between the emotions of fear and doubt, and your intuition.
- Know that by trusting your intuition you increase your chances for success.

| The Tenth Lesson |

SEEK PEACE WITHIN

A gold medal is a wonderful thing,

but if you're not enough without it,

you'll never be enough with it.

—COACH IRV BLISTER, *IN COOL RUNNINGS*

*I*t became impossible to see through the blowing snow, and I realized that one misplaced step would send me 5,000 feet into oblivion. I had to keep moving but I had slowed down to barely a crawl. I knew something was wrong with me—beyond the effects of being at 26,000 feet, in the death zone—but I didn't know what. I didn't know which way to go, so I just followed my instincts as best I could.

The wind seemed to suck the life from me. I couldn't even see my feet because of the blinding snow. The bleakness of my situation overwhelmed me as I dragged my weary, oxygen-depleted body over yet another cliff. The effort caused me to breathe so heavily, so deeply, that I felt as if I was drowning in the darkness of the night—there was simply no air to breathe. With every step I was acutely aware of the mile-long drop beneath my feet. The gale-force wind continued to batter me against the cliff as I fought to find a better way—any way—over or around the wall. Even in my thick down suit I was shivering from the −100°F wind-chill. The narrow beam from my headlamp hardly pierced the thick blowing snow, but it was all I had. I climbed up several vertical sections of rock, and then back down a few steep snow-filled gullies, desperately trying to find a way that made sense, that actually led somewhere.

Minutes passed like hours, and each hour felt like a day. I thought I was going to die. Earlier on the trip, I had been so excited to be on Everest; now I felt incredibly lonely and isolated, as if I was the only person on earth. I was tempted to sit down and give up, but I wouldn't let myself rest, since I knew stopping would mean freezing and no doubt losing fingers and toes. Worse yet, I would drift off to sleep and never wake up, though that thought seemed an almost appealing way to escape the nightmare. I desperately wanted to close my eyes and wake up back home. Just then, I came across footprints in the snow, and for a minute thought that someone else was out here looking for me, that I was saved. Then I realized—they were my footprints. I'd been walking around in a circle on this huge face.

I leaned against the rock wall, put my head in my hands and cried out: "God help me! I don't know which way to go."

I didn't hear a deep heavenly voice telling me which way to go—I simply saw Diane's face, smiling. I remember thinking, "She's not going to dig a guy without fingers or toes, and I'm not much good to her dead." It was not my life I was worried about losing; it was the thought of losing the opportunity to spend the rest of my life with Diane. She was counting on me to come home, and I didn't want to let her down! Every-thing became clear. Surviving was my only option—surviving and returning home to my soulmate was my only dream. I knew I had to keep moving. "You've got to get back to Diane," played in my head, over and over. And that alone gave me the power to turn from the cliff and push into the wind, more determined than ever to forge on to Camp Four and safety.

Soon after, the storm mysteriously calmed down and the clouds parted. Weeks later I learned that back home in the United States something very extraordinary was happening. Diane was on her knees praying for me; at exactly the same time, thou-sands of miles apart, her twin sister Donna and her older sister Lizabeth both sat up in bed and prayed for me, all three knowing something was terribly wrong. Their prayers obviously helped. Now I could see where I was going. I could just make out the sad-dle where our camp should be, and I could see the summit of Everest outlined above, seeming so close. I new now that I would not reach the roof of the world on this expedition, but my goal changed to one that I felt was in my reach: survival. In spite of my weakness and exhaustion, I pushed on toward Camp Four and soon saw something moving in the shad-ows of the night.

"Hell-oooooo!" I shouted as loud as I could. "Hell-oooooo!" Rang out a reply.

My heart leapt. The sound seemed to come from a few hundred feet away. Was it an echo, or another climber? There! A figure in the darkness ahead . . . then another. My teammates had come to look for me after being pinned down in their tent in the same storm, later telling me that they fully expected to find a frozen corpse, if they found a body at all. The guys placed an oxygen mask over my face. I was too tired to object. Immediately, warmth and energy flowed into my weakened body. The oxygen made an incredible difference and I was able to walk without stopping to gasp for breath. At 3:00 A.M., after climbing for more than twenty-two hours, I crawled into a wind-battered tent. My teammates were also in survival mode; the altitude sucking the life from them as it was from me, but at least they had the advantage of the bottled oxygen. My lungs burned and I coughed repeatedly. I was unable to eat or drink anything, and I spent a fitful few hours shivering in the corner of the tent until dawn came.

I was relieved to be in the tent but it didn't take long to realize that I would have to go down as soon as I could or I would die. There was no rescue team waiting to help me up here, and I was far too high for a *helicopter. I had made it through the storm, but to truly survive, I'd have to get back down, and quickly. My entire body ached. I wondered how I was going to even move. The rest of the team was exhausted from the distance they had come, and were planning to take a full day of rest before going for the summit. I wasn't going to ask any of them to give up their shot at Everest to help me down. It was difficult to think of leaving the safe haven of Camp Four.*

The memories of the night before haunted me, but I had no choice. Exhaustion, respiratory illness, and the onset of hypothermia plagued my body. I might have been able to go higher, but at what cost? Most deaths on Everest occur during the descent. I'd be lucky enough to get out of there alive as it was. No one lasts very long in the death zone. Staying alive was more important than reaching the summit. Everest would be there for another try, on another day.

I put on my pack, thanked the guys, wished them luck, and left. The first hundred yards out of camp were the hardest. I headed back down the face and to the site of my recent whiteout nightmare. My balance was off, and I slipped a few times, but luckily I was clipped onto the fixed rope, which kept me from plunging down the face. (This was the fixed rope I had vainly searched for in the storm the night before.) I felt like I was moving in a trance from the lack of food, water, and sleep, and the effects of the altitude on my weakened body. I descended the ropes automatically, barely conscious of each step.

It took me the entire day to climb down through the steep Geneva Spur and the Yellow Band to Camp Three. Dick, our team physician, had climbed up to the camp to see if I needed help. I was in intense pain, and more appreciative of his presence than he could ever imagine. He diagnosed me with bronchitis and high-altitude pneumonia in both lungs— no wonder I hadn't been feeling very well! I spent an agonizing night at Camp Three with a throbbing headache. I couldn't eat much, and didn't sleep at all.

The next morning we woke to Rick's voice on the radio, yelling that they had reached the summit of Everest! I was so excited for them, and so proud. I grabbed the radio and gave them my hearty congratulations. I was glad to be part of a successful expedition—having half your team make the summit is a rare accomplishment. Though I was not with them in person, I was with them in spirit, still a member of a successful team ascent. I reassured myself that I had made a difference by contributing all I could to help Rick and the team reach the summit. But I was envious; I wanted to be there with them. It had been my lifelong goal to summit Everest, and I had been so close.

Dick decided to wait for the summit team in case they needed any help. I was in no condition to stay, so I left as soon as I was packed. I reached Camp One and the top of the Khumbu icefall around noon. Usually we crossed the icefall before the sun hit it, and now I was standing at the top of it in the heat of the day, at its most active, and therefore most dangerous, time. I could stay here another night, or risk it and go down. I decided that if I had been meant to die on this mountain it would have happened back in the death zone, so I went for it. Previously it had taken me less than an hour to descend this section, but this time it took me more than six hours. Miraculously, I made it down unscathed, reaching the base of the icefall as the sun was setting. It seemed to take forever to cross the rocky terrain to base camp, and as I watched the sun go down a smile crept across my face. Everest had not defeated me!

The summit team returned to base camp the next evening and we celebrated until late. I packed up my gear the following morning and, with a whopping high-altitude hangover, said goodbye to everyone, and left.

As I headed down the valley away from Everest that day, I felt tremendously peaceful about the whole trip. It had dawned on me that *surviving* that night had been my "Everest." Alone, I had survived one of the worst storms the giant mountain could muster. I was proud of myself for forging on, for digging deep within myself to find the willpower to keep going under such extreme conditions, and for getting the load of food to the team at Camp Four. How easy it would have been to sit down and give up. It is incredible what a person can do when put to the test.

Later, I pondered the lessons from this latest adventure and realized that what had happened was supposed to happen, and I had learned what I was supposed to learn. I had learned far more about what I am made of, and what I am capable of doing, from getting through that night alive, than I ever would have learned from climbing those last few thousand feet to the summit. Victory is usually followed by celebration, but that may not teach us much. It's when things don't go our way that we learn the most about ourselves. I vowed that after spending twenty-four hours alone in a storm in the death zone I would never again complain about having a bad day. It was an incredibly liberating feeling to take the hardest lesson of my life and turn it into a positive, uplifting experience. I knew I'd never be the same again.

We all have an "Everest" to face in our lives. Whether it's a physical, mental, emotional, social, spiritual, or financial mountain before you, it's crucial always to have dreams and goals to pull you forward. But in the end, "conquering" your Everest isn't the real secret to inner peace—it's what you learn and what you become from the attempt, and how you apply that knowledge to your next mountain, to your next challenge. Although attaining the summit is a grand goal and a fantastic accomplishment, I knew deep down that it wouldn't make me a better person. I acknowledged the fact that I didn't need to prove myself to anyone but myself, that who I am is far more important than what I do.

Reaching the top of big mountains has shown me that external victories, however great, are short-lived, and always leave one wanting more. People can do incredible things with their lives and still feel unfulfilled; unfortunately, they have missed the most crucial piece of the puzzle. Whether you win three Super Bowl rings, or an Academy Award, or become the CEO of a Fortune 500 company, if you are not happy with who you are, you will never experience true inner peace. I also realized that sometimes we have to be flexible and allow our goals to change as circumstances change. I didn't have to let go of my goal to climb Everest alone in a day, but I had to realize that trip certainly wasn't the right time to follow that particular dream—and my very survival had depended on that realization.

We are born for adventure and achievement. In my opinion, the one who fails is the person who never tries to accomplish anything in the first place—better to have tried and failed than never to have tried at all. However, it is also important to pay attention to the lessons on the way. Even if you do not immediately reach your summits, your dreams, your goals, you are just as valuable, just as special, and just as great. It's having a goal to shoot for and how you grow in the process that's important, not just the result.

That trip was an unconditional success. Before Everest, I'd been chasing something elusive for most of my life. Was it recognition by peers? Desire to have my father feel proud of my accomplishments? Was it attention? Maybe it was just one of these, maybe all of them. Early in my mountaineering career, I climbed because I felt I had something to prove. Deep inside I thought, "Perhaps the next summit will bring me fulfillment. Maybe a higher or more difficult peak will erase my self-doubt and insecurity." It was a tremendous rush standing on top of a Himalayan peak, but that couldn't subdue the nagging emptiness within me. It took this spiritual, near-death experience on Everest to reveal true inner peace to me. I had almost traded my life for the summit's promise, merely to satisfy an inner hunger that no human accomplishment alone can fulfill.

Living life at the level of performance that makes us push ourselves and create adventure is an amazing feeling. I believe that we reach a level of internal peace when we are living true to our nature, internally satisfied with ourselves, busy pursuing our dreams, and operating at the upper edge of our ability. I know mountaineers who have climbed tragically to their deaths, believing that their whole self-worth depended on getting to the summit. If they didn't, they felt worthless and ashamed. They kept going in a storm or when they weren't feeling well, because ego and inner unrest wouldn't allow them to face themselves if they didn't finish. It's how you feel about yourself inside that counts, not your external accomplishments.

You will discover peace within yourself by the combination of choosing a mountain to climb, mastering your skills, lightening your load, choosing your partners wisely, conquering your fear, believing in yourself, exploring your limits, finding your pace, and following your instincts. It's a long, hard ascent, and it's certainly scary at times, but the view from the top is incredible, and besides, it's a climb you know you must attempt. These ten lessons give anyone the power to make progress toward personal and professional goals. Even if you apply one or two of these lessons to your life you'll be that much closer to achieving your goals. However, without inner peace, your achievements will feel empty. The pressures and external expectations from your occupation, your colleagues, your loved ones, and your culture in general will always be there. Coming to grips with who you are will allow you to remain true to your purpose when the storms rage and the pressures build. Life can be and should be an incredible adventure, if we follow our hearts and pursue our dreams, and so live true to ourselves.

Steps to discovering inner peace:

- ■ Strive to live true to your nature.
- ■ Push yourself to reach your full potential.
- ■ Learn as you go.
- ■ Know that you are special and unique, whether you achieve the summit or not!
- ■ Recognize that who you are is more important than what you do.

To contact Gary Scott for speaking engagements:
gary@garyscottadventures.com

For information on Gary's adventure travel trips:
www.garyscottadventures.com

OTHER BOOKS FROM
BEYOND WORDS PUBLISHING, INC.

Extreme Spirituality

Radical Journeys for the Inward Bound

Author: Tolly Burkan; Foreword: Andrew Weil, M.D.

Extreme Spirituality is accepting, even embracing, challenging situations in order to grow in spirit. By reading about more than twenty extreme spiritual practices, readers learn how even unpleasant or dangerous situations can help us experience love, wisdom, compassion, and how interconnection reveals aspects of our divine nature.

The Beatles Way

Fab Wisdom for Everyday Life

Author: Larry Lange

$14.95, softcover

Millions of people have been influenced by the Beatles' messages over the years. Anyone who has ever loved them knows they were excellent at their craft. But there was more to them than great music. They were living models of how to be who you wish to be and practice peace in life. With its seven foundations of fab and its many Beatle anecdotes, *The Beatles Way* is a fun trip that shows readers how to bring the Beatles' attitude and enthusiasm into their own lives

Your Authentic Self

Be Yourself at Work
Author: Ric Giardina
$14.95, softcover

Working people everywhere feel that they lead double lives: an "on the job" life and a personal life. Is it possible to live a life in which the separate parts of our personalities are united? In *Your Authentic Self*, author Ric Giardina explains that it is possible, and the key to achieving this integrated existence is authenticity. By honoring your authentic self at the workplace, you will not only be much happier, but you will also be rewarded with better on-the-job performance and more fulfilling work relationships. With straightforward techniques that produce instant results, this practical and easy-to-use guide will empower you to make the shift from seeing work as "off the path" of personal and spiritual growth to recognizing it as an integral part of your journey.

A Guy's Guide to Pregnancy

Preparing for Parenthood Together

Author: Frank Mungeam; Foreword: John Gray, Ph.D.

$12.95, softcover

Every day, four thousand American men become first-time dads. There are literally hundreds of pregnancy guidebooks aimed at women, but guys rarely rate more than a footnote. *A Guy's Guide to Pregnancy* is the first book to explain in "guy terms" the changes that happen to a man's partner and their relationship during pregnancy, using a humorous yet insightful approach. Future fathers will find out what to expect when they enter the "Pregnancy Zone." *A Guy's Guide to Pregnancy* is designed to be guy-friendly—approachable in appearance as well as content and length. It is divided into forty brisk chapters, one for each week of the pregnancy.

Seeing Your Life Through New Eyes

InSights to Freedom from Your Past

Authors: Paul Brenner, M.D., Ph.D., and Donna Martin, M.A.

$14.95, softcover

Seeing Your Life Through New Eyes is in a hands-on workbook format that helps you create a diary of self-discovery and assists you in resolving any misunderstood relationships. You can learn how to uncover unconscious patterns that define how you love, what you value, and what unique gifts you have in life. This book reveals those obstacles that too often interfere with loving relationships and creative expression, and it includes diagrams to use for your personal exploration and growth.

Believe to Achieve

See the Invisible, Do the Impossible
Author: Howard "H" White
$17.95 hardcover

Howard "H" White tells us: *Extraordinary people are simply ordinary people on fire with desire*—Band he knows. As NIKE, Inc.'s liaison for athletes such as Michael Jordan and Charles Barkley, "H" has had plenty of experience with superstars. But he didn't start there. He has known extraordinary people his whole life, from his family and friends to his coaches and teachers. All along the way Howard has met people who opened his eyes to his own abilities, and he's spent his life doing the same for others.

Full of behind-the-scenes moments with favorite athletes as well as funny anecdotes, *Believe to Achieve* is an exuberant collection of wisdom that will help you recognize the potential in yourself and see the path to success. It's a handbook for all people who have a goal they don't know how to reach or who want to help others discover their gifts.

To order or to request a catalog, contact

Beyond Words Publishing, Inc.
20827 N.W. Cornell Road, Suite 500
Hillsboro, OR 97124-9808
503-531-8700

You can also visit our Web site at *www.beyondword.com* or e-mail us at *info@beyondword.com.*

Beyond Words Publishing, Inc.

OUR CORPORATE MISSION

Inspire to Integrity

OUR DECLARED VALUES

We give to all of life as life has given us.
We honor all relationships.
Trust and stewardship are integral to fulfilling dreams.
Collaboration is essential to create miracles.
Creativity and aesthetics nourish the soul.
Unlimited thinking is fundamental.
Living your passion is vital.
Joy and humor open our hearts to growth.
It is important to remind ourselves of love.